$\mathcal{T}$HE

$\mathcal{I}$NDISPENSABLE

GROOM'S

$\mathcal{G}$UIDE

A handy guide containing all the
information a groom should know
when planning a wedding.

By
Elizabeth & Alex Lluch
Professional Wedding Consultants

Written by Elizabeth & Alex Lluch
Published by Wedding Solutions
© Copyright 1997, 2001

The Indispensable Groom's Guide was
Reviewed and Approved by:
Wilda Hyer,
California State Coordinator for the Association of Bridal Consultants; Owner of *Events Plus,* Ceres, California;

and

Gayle Labenow,
New York Metro Coordinator for the Association of Bridal Consultants; Owner of *You Are Cordially Invited,* Babylon, New York.

Information for *Easy Honeymoon Planner* was Researched and Compiled by:
Katherine Williams

ISBN 1-887169-16-4

$\mathcal{T}$HE WEDDING OF

_____

$\mathscr{E}$

_____

$\mathcal{W}$HO WILL BE MARRIED

ON

_____

$\mathcal{A}$T

_____

*D*edicated To:

Brandon Lee*, movie actor
and son of Bruce Lee. May he
rest in peace.

*The publisher of this book, Wedding
Solutions, was planning the wedding
of Mr. Lee when he was killed during
the filming of the movie "The Crow,"
two weeks before his wedding.

---

*P*hoto *C*redits:

Cover Photo:
Jon Barber Photography
Dana Point, CA
(949) 493-5840
www.barberphotography.com

Back Cover: (Top and Bottom)
Karen French Photography
Huntington Beach, CA
(800) 734-6219
www.karenfrenchphotography.com

Back Cover: (Middle)
Karen DiTullio Photography
Pawtucket, RI
(401) 727-2718

$\mathscr{C}$ONTENTS

Introduction	7
Wedding Planning Checklist	9
Budget Analysis	21
Financial Responsibilities	35
Wedding Party Responsibilities	37
All About Diamonds	45
Newspaper Announcements	59
Legal Matters	61
Groom's Formal Wear	65
Gifts	69
Bachelor Party	71
Rehearsal Dinner	75
Things to Bring	77
Wedding Formations	79

The Wedding Day	85
Toasts	87
Do's and Don'ts	89
Things to Do	95
Easy Honeymoon Planning	103
Other Great Wedding Products	201

*I*NTRODUCTION

D ear Groom:

Congratulations on your engagement! You must be very excited for having found that special woman to share the rest of your life with. And you must be looking forward to what will be the happiest day of your life -- your wedding! Planning your wedding can be fun and exciting. But it can also be very stressful. That is why Wedding Solutions, a professional wedding planning company, created *The Indispensable Groom's Guide*.

Now more than ever before, grooms are getting involved in the planning of their wedding. This can be very satisfying and will give you the opportunity to voice your opinion about what kind of wedding you would like to have.

The Indispensable Groom's Guide starts with a detailed checklist of things to do. This list contains everything that a groom is either responsible for or should help his fiancée with. Discuss this list with your fiancée and decide who is going to do what. Remember, planning your wedding should be a joint effort.

The book then continues with all aspects of the wedding a groom is traditionally responsible for. This book also includes a complete honeymoon planner to assist you and your bride in making your honeymoon as memorable and enjoyable as it can be.

We are confident that you will enjoy planning your wedding with the help of *The Indispensable Groom's Guide*.

If you have any comments about this book or suggestions to make, please write to us at: Wedding Solutions; 6347 Caminito Tenedor; San Diego, CA 92120 We listen to grooms like you -- that is why *The Indispensable Groom's Guide* has become an indispensable wedding guide for the groom!

Sincerely,

Alex A. Lluch
Member, Association of Bridal Consultants

Wedding

Planning

Checklist

The following Wedding Planning Checklist itemizes everything you need to do or consider when planning your wedding, and gives the best time frame in which to accomplish each activity.

This checklist assumes that you have nine months or more to plan your wedding. If your wedding is in less than nine months, just start at the beginning of the list and try to catch up as quickly as you can!

Use the boxes to the left of the items to check-off activities as you accomplish them. This will enable you to see your progress

and help you determine what has been done
and what still needs to be done.

Nine Months and Earlier

- ❑ Announce your engagement.
- ❑ Select a date for your wedding.
- ❑ Hire a professional wedding consultant.
- ❑ Determine the type of wedding you want: location, formality, time of day, number of guests, etc.
- ❑ Determine budget and how expenses will be shared.
- ❑ Develop a record-keeping system for payments made.
- ❑ Consolidate all guest lists: bride's, groom's, bride's family, groom's family, and organize as follows:

  1) those who must be invited

  2) those who should be invited

  3) those who would be nice to invite

- ❑ Decide if you want to include children among guests.
- ❑ Select and reserve ceremony site.
- ❑ Select and reserve your officiant.

☐ Select and reserve reception site.

☐ Send engagement notice with a photograph to your local newspaper.

☐ Buy a calendar and note all important activities: luncheons, parties, get-togethers, etc.

☐ If ceremony or reception is at home, arrange for home or garden improvements as needed.

☐ Order passport, visa or birth certificate, if needed for your honeymoon or marriage license.

☐ Select and book photographer.

☐ Select maid of honor, best man, bridesmaids and ushers (approx. one usher per 50 guests).

Six to Nine Months Before Wedding

☐ Select flower girl and ring bearer.

☐ Give the *Wedding Party Responsibility Cards* to your wedding party.

☐ Reserve wedding night bridal suite.

☐ Select and book caterer, if needed.

❑ Select and book ceremony musicians.

❑ Select and book reception musicians or DJ.

❑ Select and book videographer.

❑ Select and book florist.

Four to Six Months

Before Wedding

❑ Start shopping for your bride's wedding gift.

❑ Reserve rental items needed for ceremony & reception.

❑ Finalize guest list.

❑ Select and order wedding invitations, announcements and other stationery such as thank-you notes, wedding programs, and seating cards.

❑ Set date, time and location for your rehearsal dinner.

❑ Arrange accommodations for out-of-town guests.

❑ Start planning your honeymoon.

☐ Select and book all miscellaneous services, i.e. gift attendant, valet parking, etc.

☐ Register for gifts.

Two to Four Months
Before Wedding

☐ Select and order wedding cake.

☐ Order party favors.

☐ Select and order room decorations.

☐ Purchase honeymoon attire & luggage.

☐ Select and book transportation for wedding day.

☐ Check blood test and marriage license requirements.

☐ Shop for wedding rings.

☐ Consider having your teeth cleaned.

☐ Consider writing a will and/or prenuptial agreement.

☐ Plan activities for your out-of-town guests both before and after the wedding.

☐ Purchase gifts for wedding attendants.

Six to Eight Weeks
Before Wedding

- ☐ Mail invitations. Include accommodation choices and a map to assist guests in finding the ceremony and reception sites.

- ☐ Finalize shopping for wedding day accessories such as toasting glasses, ring pillow, guest book, etc.

- ☐ Check with your local newspapers for wedding announcement requirements.

- ☐ Have your formal wedding portrait taken.

- ☐ Send wedding announcement & photograph to your local newspapers.

- ☐ Select and reserve wedding attire for groom, ushers, father of the bride and ring bearer.

- ☐ Select a guest book attendant. Decide where and when to have guests sign in.

- ☐ Mail invitations to rehearsal dinner.

- ☐ Get blood test and health certificate.

☐ Obtain marriage license.

☐ Finalize your menu, beverage and alcohol order with your caterer.

Two to Six Weeks
Before Wedding

☐ Confirm ceremony details with your officiant.

☐ Finalize rehearsal dinner plans; arrange seating and write names on place cards, if desired.

☐ Make a detailed schedule for your wedding party.

☐ Make a detailed schedule for your service providers.

☐ Confirm details with all service providers, including attire. Give them a copy of your wedding schedule.

☐ Start packing for your honeymoon.

☐ Finalize addressing and stamping announcements.

☐ Decide if you want to form a receiving line. If so, determine when and where to form the line.

☐ Contact guests who haven't responded.

☐ Pick up rings and check for fit.

☐ Meet with photographer and confirm special photos you want taken.

☐ Meet with videographer and confirm special events or people you want videotaped.

☐ Meet with musicians and confirm music to be played during special events such as first dance.

☐ Remind your ushers of when and where to pick up their wedding attire.

☐ Determine ceremony seating for special guests. Give a list to the ushers.

☐ Plan reception room layout and seating with your reception site manager or caterer. Write names on place cards for arranged seating.

The Last Week

☐ Pick up wedding attire and make sure everything fits.

☐ Do final guest count and notify your caterer or reception site manager.

☐ Gather everything you will need for the rehearsal and wedding day as listed in the *Wedding Party Responsibility Cards*.

☐ Arrange for someone to drive the getaway car.

☐ Review the schedule of events and last minute arrangements with your service providers.

☐ Confirm all honeymoon reservations and accommodations. Pick up tickets and travelers checks.

☐ Finish packing your suitcases for the honeymoon.

☐ Familiarize yourself with guests' names. It will help during the receiving line and reception.

☐ Have the Post Office hold your mail while you are away on your honeymoon.

The **Rehearsal Day**

☐ Review list of things to bring to the rehearsal as listed in the *Wedding Party Responsibility Cards*.

☐ Put suitcases in getaway car.

☐ Give best man the officiant's fee and any other checks for service providers. Instruct him to deliver these checks the day of the wedding.

☐ Arrange for someone to bring accessories such as flower basket, ring pillow, guest book & pen, toasting glasses, cake cutting knife and napkins to the ceremony and reception.

☐ Arrange for someone to mail announcements the day after the wedding.

☐ Arrange for someone to return rental items such as tuxedos, slip and cake pillars after the wedding.

☐ Provide each member of your wedding party with a detailed schedule of events for the wedding day.

☐ Review ceremony seating with ushers.

*T*he Wedding Day

☐ Review list of things to bring to the ceremony as listed in the *Wedding Party Responsibility Cards.*

☐ Give the bride's ring to the best man.

☐ Simply follow your detailed schedule of events.

☐ Relax and enjoy your wedding!

BUDGET

ANALYSIS

This comprehensive Budget Analysis has been designed to provide you with all the expenses that can be incurred in any size wedding, including such hidden costs as taxes, gratuities and other "items" that can easily add up to thousands of dollars in a wedding. After you have completed this budget, you will have a clear idea of what your wedding will cost. You can then prioritize and allocate your expenses accordingly.

This budget is divided into fifteen categories: Ceremony, Wedding Attire, Photography, Videography, Stationery, Reception, Music, Bakery, Flowers, Decorations, Transportation, Rental Items, Gifts, Parties, and Miscellaneous.

At the beginning of each category, we have indicated the percentage of your wedding budget that is typically spent in each category, based on national averages. Multiply your intended wedding budget by this percentage and write that amount in the "typical" space provided.

To determine the total cost of your wedding, estimate the amount of money you will spend on each item in the budget analysis and write that amount in the "Budget" column after each item. Items printed in italics are traditionally paid for by you or your family.

Add all the "Budget" amounts within each category and write that amount in the "Budget Subtotal" space at the end of each category. Then add all the "Subtotal" figures to come up with your final wedding budget. The "Actual" column is for you to input your actual expenses as you purchase items or hire your service providers. Writing down the actual expenses will help you stay within your budget.

If you find, after adding up all your "Budget Subtotals," that the total amount is more than what you had in mind to spend, simply decide which items are more important to you and adjust your expenses accordingly.

*B*udget *A*nalysis

Your Total Wedding Budget $_____

CEREMONY

(Typical = 5% of Total Budget) $_____

	BUDGET	**ACTUAL**
Ceremony Site Fee	$_____	$_____
Officiant's Fee	$_____	$_____
Officiant's Gratuity	$_____	$_____
Guest Book, Pen, Penholder	$_____	$_____
Ring Bearer Pillow	$_____	$_____
Flower Girl Basket	$_____	$_____
Subtotal 1	$_____	$_____

WEDDING ATTIRE

(Typical = 10% of
  Total Budget) $_____

	BUDGET	ACTUAL
Bridal Gown	$_____	$_____
Alterations	$_____	$_____
Headpiece & Veil	$_____	$_____
Gloves	$_____	$_____
Jewelry	$_____	$_____
Stockings	$_____	$_____
Garter	$_____	$_____
Shoes	$_____	$_____
Hairdresser	$_____	$_____
Makeup Artist	$_____	$_____
Manicure/Pedicure	$_____	$_____
Groom's Formal Wear	$_____	$_____
Subtotal 2	$_____	$_____

PHOTOGRAPHY

(Typical = 9% of
  Total Budget) $_____

	BUDGET	ACTUAL
Bride & Groom's Album	$_____	$_____

PHOTOGRAPHY (CONT.)	BUDGET	ACTUAL
Parents' Album	$	$
Extra Prints	$	$
Proofs/Previews	$	$
Negatives	$	$
Engagement Photograph	$	$
Formal Bridal Portrait	$	$
Subtotal 3	$	$

VIDEOGRAPHY

(Typical = 5% of Total Budget) $_____

	BUDGET	ACTUAL
Main Video	$	$
Titles	$	$
Extra Hours	$	$
Photo Montage	$	$
Extra Copies	$	$
Subtotal 4	$	$

STATIONERY

(Typical = 4% of
Total Budget)

$_____

	BUDGET	ACTUAL
Invitations	$_____	$_____
Response Cards	$_____	$_____
Reception Cards	$_____	$_____
Ceremony Cards	$_____	$_____
Pew Cards	$_____	$_____
Seating/Place Cards	$_____	$_____
Rain Cards	$_____	$_____
Maps	$_____	$_____
Ceremony Programs	$_____	$_____
Announcements	$_____	$_____
Thank-You Notes	$_____	$_____
Stamps	$_____	$_____
Calligraphy	$_____	$_____
Napkins and Matchbooks	$_____	$_____
Subtotal 5	$_____	$_____

RECEPTION

(Typical = 35% of Total Budget)	$_____	
	BUDGET	**ACTUAL**
Reception Site Fee	$_____	$_____
Hors D' Oeuvres	$_____	$_____
Main Meal/Caterer	$_____	$_____
Liquor/ Beverages	$_____	$_____
Bartending/Bar Set-up Fee	$_____	$_____
Corkage Fee	$_____	$_____
Pour Coffee	$_____	$_____
Service Providers' Meals	$_____	$_____
Gratuity	$_____	$_____
Party Favors	$_____	$_____
Disposable Cameras	$_____	$_____
Rose Petals/Rice	$_____	$_____
Gift Attendant	$_____	$_____
Parking Fee/Valet Services	$_____	$_____
Subtotal 6	$_____	$_____

MUSIC

(Typical = 5% of Total Budget) $_____

	BUDGET	ACTUAL
Ceremony Music	$_____	$_____
Reception Music	$_____	$_____
Subtotal 7	$_____	$_____

BAKERY

(Typical = 2% of Total Budget) $_____

	BUDGET	ACTUAL
Wedding Cake	$_____	$_____
Groom's Cake	$_____	$_____
Cake Delivery & Set-up Fee	$_____	$_____
Cake-Cutting Fee	$_____	$_____
Cake Top	$_____	$_____
Cake Knife/Toast Glasses	$_____	$_____
Subtotal 8	$_____	$_____

FLOWERS

(Typical = 6% of Total Budget)	$_____	
	BUDGET	**ACTUAL**

BOUQUETS

Bride's	$_____	$_____
Tossing	$_____	$_____
Maid of Honor's	$_____	$_____
Bridesmaids'	$_____	$_____

FLORAL HAIRPIECE

Maid of Honor/ Bridesmaids'	$_____	$_____
Flower Girl's	$_____	$_____

CORSAGES

Bride's Going Away	$_____	$_____
Other Family Members'	$_____	$_____

BOUTONNIERES

Groom's	$_____	$_____
Ushers and Other Family's	$_____	$_____

FLOWERS (CONT.)	BUDGET	ACTUAL
CEREMONY SITE FLOWERS		
Main Altar	$_____	$_____
Alter Candelabra	$_____	$_____
Aisle Pews	$_____	$_____
RECEPTION SITE FLOWERS		
Reception Site	$_____	$_____
Head Table	$_____	$_____
Guest Tables	$_____	$_____
Buffet Table	$_____	$_____
Punch Table	$_____	$_____
Cake Table	$_____	$_____
Cake	$_____	$_____
Cake Knife	$_____	$_____
Toasting Glasses	$_____	$_____
Floral Delivery & Setup	$_____	$_____
Subtotal 9	$_____	$_____

DECORATIONS

(Typical = 3% of
Total Budget)

$ _____

	BUDGET	ACTUAL
Table Centerpieces	$_____	$_____
Balloons	$_____	$_____
Subtotal 10	$_____	$_____

TRANSPORTATION

(Typical = 2% of
Total Budget)

$ _____

	BUDGET	ACTUAL
Transportation	$_____	$_____
Subtotal 11	$_____	$_____

RENTAL ITEMS

(Typical = 3% of
Total Budget)

$ _____

	BUDGET	ACTUAL
Bridal Slip	$_____	$_____
Ceremony Accessories	$_____	$_____
Tent/Canopy	$_____	$_____
Dance Floor	$_____	$_____

RENTAL ITEMS (CONT.)	BUDGET	ACTUAL
Tables/Chairs	$_____	$_____
Linen/Tableware	$_____	$_____
Heaters	$_____	$_____
Lanterns	$_____	$_____
Other	$_____	$_____
Subtotal 12	$_____	$_____

GIFTS

(Typical = 3% of Total Budget)	$_____	
	BUDGET	ACTUAL
Bride's Gift	$_____	$_____
Groom's Gift	$_____	$_____
Bridesmaids' Gifts	$_____	$_____
Ushers' Gifts	$_____	$_____
Subtotal 13	$_____	$_____

PARTIES

(Typical = 4% of Total Budget) $ _____

	BUDGET	ACTUAL
Bridesmaids' Luncheon	$ _____	$ _____
Rehearsal Dinner	$ _____	$ _____
Subtotal 14	$ _____	$ _____

MISCELLANEOUS

(Typical = 4% of Total Budget) $ _____

	BUDGET	ACTUAL
Newspaper Announcement	$ _____	$ _____
Marriage License	$ _____	$ _____
Prenuptial Agreement	$ _____	$ _____
Bridal Gown Preservation	$ _____	$ _____
Bouquet Preservation	$ _____	$ _____
Wedding Consultant	$ _____	$ _____
Wedding Planning Software	$ _____	$ _____
Taxes	$ _____	$ _____
Subtotal 15	$ _____	$ _____

TOTAL (Add $_____ $_____
"Budget" & "Actual"
Subtotals 1-15")

FINANCIAL RESPONSIBILITIES

The following are the typical financial responsibilities for you, your family and your attendants.

Groom and/or Groom's Family

- Own travel expenses and attire
- Rehearsal dinner
- Bride's gift
- Bride's wedding ring
- Gifts for groom's attendants
- Medical exam for groom including blood test
- Bride's bouquet and going away corsage
- Mothers' and grandmothers' corsages
- All boutonnieres
- Officiant's fee
- Marriage license
- Honeymoon expenses
- Groom's Cake

♦   Prenuptial agreement

Groom's Attendants

♦   Own attire except flowers
♦   Travel expenses
♦   Bachelor party paid for by best man and ushers

WEDDING PARTY

RESPONSIBILITIES

Each member of your wedding party has his/her own individual duties and responsibilities. The following is a list of the most important duties for each member of your wedding party.

The best and most convenient method of conveying this information to members of your wedding party is by purchasing a set of the *Wedding Party Responsibility Cards* published by Wedding Solutions.

These cards are very attractive and contain all the information your wedding party needs to know to assure a smooth wedding; i.e., what to do, how to do it, when to do it, when to arrive, and much more. They also include Financial Responsibilities as well as the Processional, Recessional and Altar line-ups.

These cards are available at most major bookstores. You can also order them on-line at YourBridalSuperstore.com.

BEST MAN

- Responsible for organizing ushers' activities.
- Organizes bachelor party for groom.
- Drives groom to ceremony site and sees that he is properly dressed before the wedding.
- Arrives dressed at ceremony site 1 hour before the wedding for photographs.
- Brings marriage license to wedding.
- Pays the clergyman, musicians, photographer, and any other service providers the day of the wedding.
- Holds the bride's ring for the groom, if no ring bearer, until needed by officiant.
- Witnesses the signing of the marriage license.
- Drives newlyweds to reception if no hired driver.
- Offers first toast at reception, usually before dinner.
- Keeps groom on schedule.
- Dances with maid of honor during the bridal party dance.

- May drive couple to airport or honeymoon suite.
- Oversees return of tuxedo rentals for groom and ushers, on time and in good condition.

$\mathscr{U}$SHERS

- Help best man with bachelor party.
- Arrive dressed at ceremony site 1 hour before the wedding for photographs.
- Distribute wedding programs and maps to the reception as guests arrive.
- Seat guests at the ceremony as follows:
  - -- If female, offer the right arm.
  - -- If male, walk along his left side.
  - -- If couple, offer right arm to female; male follows a step or two behind.
  - -- Seat bride's guests in left pews.
  - -- Seat groom's guests in right pews.
  - -- Maintain equal number of guests in left and right pews, if possible.
  - -- Should a group of guests arrive at the same time, seat the eldest woman first.
  - -- Just prior to the processional, escort groom's mother to her seat; then escort bride's mother to her seat.
- Two ushers may roll carpet down the aisle after both mothers are seated.
- If pew ribbons are used, two ushers may loosen them one row at a time after the ceremony.

- Direct guests to the reception site.
- Dance with bridesmaids and other important guests.

GROOM'S MOTHER

- Helps prepare guest list for groom and his family.
- Selects attire that complements mother of the bride's attire.
- Makes accommodations for groom's out-of-town guests.
- With groom's father, plans rehearsal dinner.
- Arrives dressed at ceremony site 1 hour before the wedding for photographs.
- May stand up to signal the start of the processional.
- Can witness the signing of the marriage license.

Groom's Father

- Helps prepare guest list for groom and his family.
- Selects attire that complements groom's attire.
- With groom's mother, plans rehearsal dinner.
- Offers toast to bride at rehearsal dinner.
- Arrives dressed at ceremony site 1 hour before the wedding for photographs.
- Can witness the signing of the marriage license.

ALL ABOUT

DIAMONDS

Throughout the world, diamonds are used to symbolize love and the unbreakable bond of marriage. Searching for a diamond, however, can be very stressful since there are many factors that can affect your decision, such as shape, size, beauty and cost. The following information will give you the knowledge you need to make that very special purchase.

DIAMOND SHAPES

There are various shapes of diamonds. The most popular is the round cut, known as "brilliant." Close to 75 percent of diamonds sold are round. This is mainly because they tend to sparkle more than the other shapes. Other shapes, such as marquise, oval, emerald, princess (or square), and the pear shape, are known as "fancy."

BEFORE YOU BUY

Before purchasing a diamond, you will need to know your fiancée's taste. If you are planning to surprise your fiancée, try to purchase your diamond from a reputable source that offers a money back guarantee or at least allows exchange.

DIAMOND LINGO

Boat: The boat is a piece of paper used to hold the diamond upright (in a V-shape) so one can look at the diamond. This paper is extremely white so it allows you to see the diamond's true color.

Brilliance: Brilliance is the amount of sparkle a diamond possesses.

Chips: Chips are external nicks in the girdle of the diamond.

Clouds: Clouds refer to a cloudy area inside the diamond.

Crown: The crown is the part of the diamond above the girdle.

Culet: The culet is the minute bottom facet of the stone.

Facets: Facets are the planes on a diamond which direct light through the stone.

Feathers: Feathers are used to describe a central crack with little cracks along its side.

Fire: Fire is the intensity of colors created by a diamond.

Girdle: The girdle is the rim or edge of the stone having the largest diameter.

Inclusions: Inclusions are the carbon spots inside a diamond which reflect light, making the spot look black.

Scratch: A scratch is a mark on the face of the diamond. Scratches can usually be polished out.

Pavilion: The pavilion is the part of the diamond below the girdle.

Table: The table is the broad top facet of the diamond.

Drawing of
DIAMOND

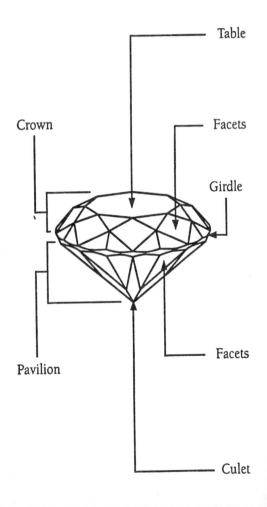

Table

Crown

Facets

Girdle

Pavilion

Facets

Culet

THE FOUR C's

The famous four C's are the main characteristics that determine the value of a diamond.
They refer to color, cut, clarity and carat.

Color

A diamond's color scale ranges from D to Z.

D to F:	Colorless
G to J:	Near colorless
K to M:	Faint yellow
N to R:	Very light yellow
S to Z:	Light yellow
Z+:	Fancy or colored

Keep in mind that the slight color of near
colorless diamonds is usually visible only
through a magnifying lens and from the un-
derside of the diamond. Therefore, minor
shades of color, even in diamonds in the I
category, are hard to see in mounted stones.

Cut

Cut is the most important element of a diamond. It is what gives the diamond fire and sparkle. Most women would agree that a smaller diamond with a lot of fire and sparkle is better than a bigger diamond without any flair.

A diamond that is cut too shallow may appear larger than a properly cut diamond of the same size, but it may have less sparkle. On the other hand, a diamond that is cut too deep may appear smaller than a properly cut diamond of the same size, but it may look darker.

Prices can vary as much as 50 percent between a well-cut stone and a poorly-cut stone.

Clarity

The clarity of the diamond is also very important as it allows you to see the diamond's level of perfection. The more imperfections in a diamond, the less fire or sparkle it has. The less imperfections in a diamond, the more light that can pass through it.

Clarity is graded on a scale of Flawless (FL), Internally Flawless (IF), Very Very Slight Inclusion (VVS1 and VVS2), Very Slight Inclusion (VSl and VS2), and Slight Inclusion (SI1-SI3). Clarity is always graded under a jeweler's loupe (10x magnification) and always with an experienced eye.

Flaws or Inclusions

All diamonds have one or more inclusions, whether visible or not, but no two diamonds have the same inclusion in the same area. Therefore, flaws or inclusions are often referred to as the "fingerprint" of the diamond.

Flawless (FL)

An FL diamond contains no imperfections. These diamonds are extremely rare and therefore very expensive.

Internally flawless (IF)

An IF diamond has no internal inclusions and very few minor external inclusions.

Very Very Slight Inclusions (VVS1)

A VVS1 diamond has very small inclusions, mainly externally. These inclusions are so
small that they are hard to find even with a jeweler's loupe.

Very Very Slight Inclusions (VVS2)

A VVS2 diamond has a little larger inclusion than the VVS1 but it is still hard to see under a jeweler's loupe.

Very Slight Inclusions 1 (VS1)

A VS1 diamond has small inclusions, usually around the edge of the stone. It is not easy to see these inclusions under a jeweler's loupe.

Very Slight Inclusions 2 (VS2)

A VS2 diamond has small inclusions, usually around the heart of the stone. These inclusions may be a little difficult to see under a jeweler's loupe.

Slight Inclusions 1 (SI1)

An SI1 diamond has few inclusions, usually around the edge of the diamond. These inclusions are easy to locate under a jeweler's loupe.

Slight Inclusions 2 (SI2)

An SI2 diamond has inclusions, usually around the table of the diamond. These inclusions are very easy to locate under a jeweler's loupe.

Slight Inclusions 3 (SI3)

An SI3 diamond has inclusions, usually under the table of the diamond. These inclusions are very easy to locate under a jeweler's loupe.

Inclusions 1 (I1)

An I1 diamond has several inclusions inside the diamond that are very easy to locate under a jeweler's loupe and may even be seen with the naked eye.

Inclusions 2 (I2)

An I2 diamond has several inclusions, usually in the heart of the stone. These inclusions are easily seen by the naked eye.

Inclusions 3 (I3)

An I3 diamond has several inclusions that are very easily seen by the naked eye.

Carat

Carat is the unit used to measure the weight of a diamond. It is equal to 200 milligrams or 142 carats to the ounce. The cost of a diamond increases exponentially as its size or weight increases. For example, a two-carat diamond costs much more than two one-carat diamonds. This is because bigger diamonds are harder to find.

The price point for a carat is about .85-carat. This means that a .80 carat diamond will cost much less than a .90 carat diamond, but a .90 carat diamond will cost almost the same as a 1 carat diamond. So if you have the choice, buy either a .80 carat diamond or, if you can afford it, a 1 carat diamond.

To save money, set a small side diamond on each side of the center diamond; this will make the center stone look much bigger. Or buy an oval diamond, which is the least expensive shape. Buy your diamond after Christmas or Valentine's Day to take advantage of sales. Summer is also a good time to buy a diamond since jewelers are usually slow during this time.

Keep in mind that color is not too crucial since it is difficult to discern color differences once the diamond is mounted.

Beware of buying a diamond from a fly-by-night operation. Buy from a reputable jeweler who offers a money-back guarantee or at least gives you the option of trading-in your diamond for another one. And make your purchase subject to verification of GIA certification.

Do not rely on verification by a GIA-certified agent recommended by the jeweler who sold you the diamond. Try to find an independent agent or go directly to the GIA. The GIA is the only independent organization which will tell you the true, unbiased characteristics of your diamond without having an interest in selling you something.

Before You Buy

Before you purchase a diamond, make sure you get a detailed appraisal of the diamond in writing. Also get in writing any other policy such as money-back or trade-in as well as whether the purchase is subject to verification of GIA certification.

When shopping for a diamond, use the following tables to compare diamonds from various sources.

*D*IAMOND
COMPARISON CHART

	Source 1	Source 2
Name of Source		
Color		
Cut		
Clarity		
Carat		
Cost	$	$

	Source 3	Source 4
Name of Source		
Color		
Cut		
Clarity		
Carat		
Cost	$	$

$\mathscr{D}$IAMOND
COMPARISON CHART

	Source 5	Source 6
Name of Source		
Color		
Cut		
Clarity		
Carat		
Cost	$	$

	Source 7	Source 8
Name of Source		
Color		
Cut		
Clarity		
Carat		
Cost	$	$

Personal Notes

NEWSPAPER

ANNOUNCEMENTS

There are two types of announcements you can send to your local newspaper: one to announce your engagement, and one to announce your wedding.

For your engagement announcement, send information to the newspapers, along with a photograph, right after your engagement or at least 4 to 6 weeks before the wedding. The photograph is usually the head and shoulders of the engaged couple.

The photograph should be wallet-sized or larger, black and white, and glossy. Call your local newspapers to ask about their requirements. Most papers will not take orders over the phone, so you will need to mail the information or deliver it personally.

For your wedding announcement, send information to the newspapers, along with a photograph of either the bride alone or both of you together, at least three weeks before the wedding. The photograph should be wallet-sized or larger, black and white, and glossy. Your photograph should show the way you will look the day of your wedding. The announcement should appear the day following the ceremony.

If you and your fiancée grew up in different towns, consider sending announcements to the local papers of both towns. If either of you is having second thoughts about the wedding, cancel both announcements as soon as possible.

If you don't mind having your wedding announced a few weeks after the wedding, you can send a photo from your actual wedding day. This will save you the cost and hassle of dressing up to have your photo taken before the wedding.

*L*EGAL

*M*ATTERS

MARRIAGE LICENSE

Marriage license requirements are state-regulated and may be obtained from the County Clerk in most county courthouses.

Some states (California and Nevada, for example) offer two types of marriage licenses: a public license and a confidential one. The public license is the most common one and requires a health certificate. This license can only be obtained at the County Clerk's office.

The confidential license is usually less expensive and does not require a health certificate. If offered, it can usually be obtained from most Justices of the Peace. An oath must be taken in order to receive either license.

Requirements vary from state to state but generally include the following points:

1. Applying for and paying the fee for the marriage license. There is usually a waiting period before the license is valid and a limited time before it expires.

2. Meeting residency requirements of the state and/or county where the ceremony will take place.

3. Meeting the legal age requirements for both bride and groom or having parental consent.

4. Presenting any required identification, birth or baptismal certificates, marriage eligibility or other documents.

5. Obtaining a medical examination and/or blood test for both the bride and groom to detect communicable diseases.

PRENUPTIAL AGREEMENT

A prenuptial agreement is a legal contract between the bride and groom itemizing the property each brings into the marriage and explaining how those properties will be divided in case of divorce or death. Although you can write your own agreement, it is advisable to have an attorney draw up or review the document. The two of you should be represented by different attorneys.

Consider a prenuptial agreement if one or both of you have a significant amount of capital or assets, or if there are children involved from a previous marriage. If you are going to live in a different state after your wedding, consider having an attorney from that state draw up or review your document.

Nobody likes to talk about divorce or death when planning a wedding, but it is very important to give these issues your utmost consideration. By drawing a prenuptial agreement, you encourage open communication and may get a better idea of each other's needs and expectations. Also consider drawing up or reviewing your wills at this time.

Some software packages allow you to write your own will and prenuptial agreement, which will save you substantial attorney's fees. However, if you decide to draw either agreement on your own, you should still have an attorney review it.

PERSONAL

NOTES

$\mathscr{G}$ROOM'S $\mathscr{F}$ORMAL $\mathscr{W}$EAR

You should select your formal wear based on the place, time and formality of your wedding. For a semi-formal or formal wedding, you will need a tuxedo. A tuxedo is the formal jacket worn by men on special or formal occasions. The most popular colors are black, white, and gray. Use the following guidelines to select customary attire for your wedding:

Informal wedding:	Business suit. White dress shirt and tie.
Semi-formal daytime:	Formal suit. White dress shirt. Cummerbund or vest. Four-in-hand or bow tie.
Semi-formal evening:	Formal suit or dinner jacket. Matching trousers. White shirt.

Cummerbund or vest.
Black bow tie. Cufflinks
and studs.

Formal daytime: Cutaway or stroller jacket.
Waistcoat. Striped
trousers. White wing-
Collared shirt. Striped tie.
Studs and cufflinks.

Formal evening: Black dinner jacket.
Matching trousers.
Waistcoat. White tuxedo
shirt. Bow tie. Cummer-
bund or vest. Cufflinks.

Very formal daytime: Cutaway coat. Wing-
collared shirt. Ascot.
Striped trousers.
Cufflinks. Gloves.

Very formal evening: Black tailcoat. Matching
striped trousers. Bow tie.
White wing-collared shirt.
Waistcoat. Patent leather
shoes. Studs and cuff-
links. Gloves.

In selecting your formal wear, keep in mind
the formality and time of day of your wedding, the bride's gown, and colors of the
bridesmaids' dresses. Consider darker colors
for a fall or winter wedding and lighter

colors for a spring or summer wedding. When selecting a place to rent your tuxedo, check the reputation of the shop. Make sure they have a wide variety of makes and styles to choose from.

Reserve tuxedos for yourself and your ushers several weeks before the wedding to insure a wide selection and to allow enough time for alterations. Plan to pick up the tuxedos a few days before the wedding to allow time for last minute alterations in case they don't fit properly. Out-of-town men in your wedding party can be sized at any tuxedo shop. They can send their measurements to you or directly to the shop where you are going to rent your tuxedos.

Ask about the store's return policy and be sure you delegate to the appropriate person (usually your best man) the responsibility of returning all tuxedos within the time allotted. Ushers customarily pay for their own tuxedos.

Try to negotiate getting your tuxedo for free or at a discount in exchange for having your father, your fiancée's father and your ushers rent their tuxedos at that shop.

PERSONAL

NOTES

GIFTS

BRIDE'S GIFT

The bride's gift is traditionally given by the groom to the bride. It is typically a personal gift such as a piece of jewelry.

A string of pearls, a watch, pearl earrings, or a gold chain with a heart-shaped charm holding photos of the two of you are nice options for a bridal gift.

To save money, consider omitting this gift altogether. This gift is not necessary and should be given only if the budget allows it. A pretty card proclaiming your eternal love for your bride is a very special yet inexpensive gift.

USHERS' GIFTS

Ushers' gifts are the gifts given by the groom to his ushers as a permanent keepsake of the wedding.

For ushers' gifts, consider fancy pen sets, wallets, leather belts, silver frames, watches, and desk clocks.

Or negotiate with your photographer to take, at no extra charge, professional portraits of each attendant and their escort for use as attendants' gifts. Select a beautiful background, such as your cake table, that will remind your attendants of the occasion. This makes a special yet inexpensive gift for your attendants.

You should deliver your gifts to the ushers at the bachelor party or at the rehearsal dinner. Your gift to the best man may be similar to the ushers' gifts but should be a bit more expensive.

$\mathscr{B}$ACHELOR

$\mathscr{P}$ARTY

The bachelor party is a men-only affair typically organized by your best man. He is responsible for selecting the date and reserving the place and entertainment as well as inviting your male friends and family. Your best man should also assign responsibilities to your ushers as they should help with the organization of the bachelor party.

You often hear wild stories about bachelor parties being nights full of loose women, alcohol, and great fun. However, these stories are actually quite rare. Most of the time, they are all lies or a big exaggeration of what really happened. It is not uncommon for the guys invited to the bachelor party to create these wild stories and make a vow of never telling the truth about how boring the party really was!

Your typical bachelor party starts with your male friends getting together for dinner and drinking a fair amount of beer. After eating and drinking to their heart's content, they may then go bar-hopping or get together at someone's house to play games or watch X-rated movies.

Going to nude dancing locations is also popular. So is hiring a call girl to go to a designated location -- either a restaurant or house. She will come prepared to strip dance in front of you. She may get your imagination to run wild, but don't get any ideas. Most strippers will only allow you to look, not touch!

Your best man should never plan your bachelor party for the night before the wedding, since chances are that you will consume a large amount of alcohol and stay up late. You don't want to have a hangover or be exhausted during your wedding. Therefore, it is much more appropriate to have the bachelor party two or three days before the wedding. You should tell your best man that you will be busy the night before the wedding, just in case he is planning to surprise you.

Your best man should designate a driver for you and for those who will drink too much. You don't want to get into an accident days before the wedding or spend your wedding day in jail for drunk driving.   Remember, you and your best man are responsible for the well-being of everybody invited to the party.

Whatever you do, make this party a memorable one! Many people do not remember their bachelor party because it was just a typical get-together with friends. Make sure you do something different and enjoy it!

One word of advice: Even though the bachelor party is your last night out as a single man, it does not give you the right to cheat on your fiancée or do something that would upset her. This would be the worst way to begin your married life.

PERSONAL

NOTES

REHEARSAL DINNER

The groom's parents customarily host a dinner party following the rehearsal, the evening before the wedding.   The dinner usually includes the bridal party, their spouses or guests, both sets of parents, close family members, the officiant, and the wedding consultant and/or coordinator.

The rehearsal dinner party can be held just about anywhere, from a restaurant, hotel, or private hall to the groom's parents' home. Close relatives and out-of-town guests may be included if the budget permits.

Restaurants specializing in Mexican food or pizza are fun yet inexpensive options for a casual rehearsal dinner.

PERSONAL

NOTES

*T*HINGS TO

*B*RING

TO THE REHEARSAL:

- Bride's gift (if not already given)
- Marriage license
- Ushers' gifts (if not already given)
- Service providers' fees to give to best man or wedding consultant so s/he can pay them at the wedding

TO THE CEREMONY:

- Airline tickets
- Announcements
- Aspirin/Alka Seltzer
- Breath spray/mints
- Bride's ring
- Change of clothes for going away
- Cologne
- Cuff Links
- Cummerbund

- Deodorant
- Hair comb
- Hair spray
- Kleenex
- Lint brush
- Luggage
- Neck tie
- Passport
- Shirt
- Shoes
- Socks
- Toothbrush & paste
- Tuxedo
- Underwear

WEDDING

FORMATIONS

The following section illustrates the typical ceremony formations (Processional, Recessional and Altar Line Up) for both Christian and Jewish weddings, as well as the typical formations for the Receiving Line, Head Table, and Parents' Tables at the reception.

These ceremony formations are included in the *Wedding Party Responsibility Cards,* published by Wedding Solutions. This attractive set of cards makes it very easy for your wedding party to remember their place in these formations. Give one card to each member of your wedding party -- they will appreciate it!

Wedding Party Responsibility Cards are available at most major bookstores or can be ordered online in the Wedding Planners section at YourBridalSuperstore.com.

CHRISTIAN CEREMONY

PROCESSIONAL

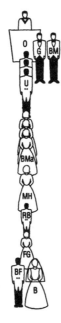

RECESSIONAL

ABBREVIATIONS

B = Bride

G = Groom

BM = Best Man

MH = Maid of Honor

BF = Bride's Father

BMo = Bride's Mother

GF = Groom's Father

GM = Groom's Mother

BMa = Bridesmaids

U = Ushers

FG = Flower Girl

RB = Ring Bearer

O = Officiant

CHRISTIAN CEREMONY

ALTAR LINE UP

Bride's Pews	Groom's Pews

ABBREVIATIONS

B = Bride
G = Groom
BM = Best Man
MH = Maid of Honor
BF = Bride's Father
BMo = Bride's Mother

GF = Groom's Father
GM = Groom's Mother
BMa = Bridesmaids
U = Ushers
FG = Flower Girl
RB = Ring Bearer
O = Officiant

JEWISH CEREMONY

PROCESSIONAL

RECESSIONAL

ABBREVIATIONS

B = Bride
G = Groom
BM = Best Man
MH = Maid of Honor
BF = Bride's Father
BMo = Bride's Mother

GF = Groom's Father
GM = Groom's Mother
BMa = Bridesmaids
U = Ushers
FG = Flower Girl
RB = Ring Bearer
R = Rabbi

JEWISH CEREMONY

ALTAR LINE UP

Groom's Pews	Bride's Pews

ABBREVIATIONS

B = Bride
G = Groom
BM = Best Man
MH = Maid of Honor
BF = Bride's Father
BMo = Bride's Mother

GF = Groom's Father
GM = Groom's Mother
BMa = Bridesmaids
U = Ushers
FG = Flower Girl
RB = Ring Bearer
R = Rabbi

RECEIVING LINE

HEAD TABLE

PARENTS' TABLE

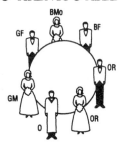

ABBREVIATIONS

B = Bride	GF = Groom's Father
G = Groom	GM = Groom's Mother
BM = Best Man	BMa = Bridesmaids
MH = Maid of Honor	U = Ushers
BF = Bride's Father	OR = Other Relatives
BMo = Bride's Mother	O = Officiant

THE

WEDDING DAY

Finally, all the months of planning and preparation have come to an end! Your wedding day is supposed to be the happiest day of your life, and you should enjoy it. This is the day to forget all arguments or misunderstandings with your fiancée and/or family members.

This is the day to be in a great mood. All attention will be focused on you and your fiancée. If you are in a bad mood or are unhappy, hundreds of photographs will reflect that. So this is the time to play politics and smile a lot.

Don't make any other plans for the wedding day. You don't want to be anxious about running out of time or being late to your own wedding. All last-minute errands and chores should be designated to a family member or member of your wedding party.

If you are nervous, ask your best man to help you relax by rubbing your shoulders or telling jokes. Do not drink before the wedding. Nothing gives a worst impression than a tipsy groom or a groom with alcohol on his breath.

Study the list of things to bring to the wedding, found on page 77. If you have not already done so, give your best man the bride's ring as well as the payments to your officiant and other service providers who will need to get paid that day.

Make sure you arrive in plenty of time at the ceremony site. There is nothing that causes more anxiety than being late to your own wedding. Have your best man check with your ushers to make sure they know where to go and at what time to arrive.

This is a day to enjoy and be happy. Remember, the main objective of this day is to marry your fiancée. If something goes wrong, don't let it bother you. Chances are that no one will notice it but yourself.

The best advise we can give you is to relax, loosen up and enjoy your wedding!

$\mathcal{T}$OASTS

It is customary for your best man to offer a toast at the reception to introduce himself, the wedding party and the newly married couple. This is followed by the groom's thanking his best man and then toasting his bride and both sets of parents.

After the groom's toast, anybody else can offer a toast. Typically, the father of the bride and the maid of honor offer a toast.

The toast begins after the receiving line breaks up at a cocktail reception or before dinner during a dinner reception. Toasts can also be offered after the main course or after the cake is served.

Your toast could be to express thanks to everybody involved in planning the wedding, to give thanks to those who traveled long distances to come to your wedding, or to give any other kind of information. It can be serious, such as expressing how much you love your new wife; or it can be funny, such as describing how your fiancée played "hard to get" when you two first met.

Your toast should not be so short that it sounds rude, or so long that your guests get bored. During the toast, everyone rises except those who are being toasted. And no one should drink from their cup until after the toast. After you finish your toast, raise your glass toward the person or persons being toasted.

Your toast should sound sincere and not rehearsed. However, it is a good idea to practice it beforehand. If you are anxious about speaking in public, you may want to join your local Toastmaster's Club. This is an organization which helps people develop confidence in public speaking.

$\mathcal{D}$O'S & $\mathcal{D}$ON'TS

Your wedding will last only a few hours but will likely take several months to plan. That is why it is so important to enjoy the complete wedding planning process. This is a time to get excited, to fall even more deeply in love with each other, to learn more about each other, and how to give and take. If you can handle your wedding planning with your fiancée and parents, you can handle anything! Here is a list of do's and don'ts when planning your special day. If you follow these suggestions, your wedding planning will be more enjoyable and the wedding itself will be much more smooth and beautiful.

DO'S

Read this book completely.

Hire a professional wedding consultant.

Maintain a sense of humor.

Maintain open communication with your fiancée and both sets of parents, especially if they are financing the wedding.

Be receptive to your parents' ideas, especially if they are financing the wedding.

Be flexible.

Keep your overall budget in mind.

Maintain a regular routine of exercise.

Eat a well-balanced diet.

Buy the *Wedding Party Responsibility Cards*, published by Wedding Solutions, and give one to each member of your wedding party.

Read *Easy Wedding Planning* or *Easy Wedding Planning Plus*, published by Wedding Solutions.

Register for gifts; consider a price range that your guests can afford.

Break-in your shoes well before your wedding day.

Check recent references for all of your service providers.

Get everything in writing with your service providers.

Assign your guests to tables and group them together by age, interest, acquaintances, etc.

Consider drawing-up a prenuptial agreement and a will.

Give a rose to each of your mothers as you walk down the aisle during the recessional.

Try to spend some time with each of your guests and personally thank them for coming to your wedding.

Encourage the bride's parents to introduce their family and friends to the family and friends of the groom's family, and vice-versa.

Toast both sets of parents at the rehearsal dinner and/or at the reception. Thank them for everything they have done and for giving you a beautiful wedding.

Eat at the reception, especially if you will be drinking alcohol.

Keep a smile on your face; there will be many photographs taken of you.

Preserve the top tier of your wedding cake for your first year anniversary.

Expect things to go wrong on your wedding day. Most likely something will go wrong, and no one will notice it but yourself. Relax and don't let it bother you.

Send a special gift to both sets of parents, such as a small album containing the best photographs of the wedding. Personalize this gift by having it engraved with your names and the date of your wedding.

DON'TS

Don't get involved in other activities; you will be very busy planning your wedding.

Don't make any major decisions without discussing them openly with your fiancée.

Don't be controlling. Be open to other people's ideas.

Don't overspend your budget; this can be extremely stressful.

Don't wait until the last minute to hire your service providers. The good ones get booked months in advance.

Don't try to make everybody happy; it is impossible and will make your life miserable.

Don't try to impress your friends.

Don't invite old girlfriends to your wedding; you don't want to make your bride feel uncomfortable.

Don't try to do "everything." Delegate responsibilities to your fiancée, your parents, and to members of your wedding party.

Don't rely on friends or family to take your wedding photographs.

Don't assume that members of your wedding party know what to do. Give each of them a copy of the *Wedding Party Responsibility Cards*, available at most major bookstores or in the Wedding Planners section at YourBridalSuperstore.com

Don't assume that your service providers know what to do.

Don't schedule your bachelor party the night before the wedding. You don't want to have a hangover on your special day.

Don't arrive late to the ceremony!

Don't get drunk at your wedding; you don't want to make a fool of yourself on your most special day.

Don't flirt with members of the opposite sex.

Don't allow your guests to drive drunk after the reception; you may be held responsible.

Don't rub cake in your bride's face during the cake-cutting ceremony; she might not appreciate it!

Don't overeat; this may upset your stomach or make you sleepy.

Don't leave your reception without saying good-bye to your family and friends.

Don't drive if you have had too much to drink.

THINGS TO DO

DONE
✓

THINGS TO DO

DONE
✓

THINGS TO DO

DONE
✓

Things To Do

DONE
✓

THINGS TO DO

DONE
✓

Things To Do

DONE
✓

THINGS TO DO

DONE
✓

$\mathcal{E}$ASY

HONEYMOON

$\mathcal{P}$LANNING

A comprehensive guide
containing all the information
a bride and groom
should know when
planning a Honeymoon.

*C*ONTENTS

Introduction	107
Types of Honeymoons	109
Traditional Honeymoons	110
Less-Traditional Honeymoons	115
Choosing Your Destination	117
Creating A Wish List	119
Helpful Resources	131
Creating a Budget	151
Tipping Guide	167
Things to Pack	171
Packing Checklist	173
International Travel	183
Passports and Visas	185
Health Concerns	191
Other Concerns	193

Things To Do   195

Other Great Wedding Products   201

*I*NTRODUCTION

Your honeymoon is the time to celebrate your new life together as a married couple. It should be the vacation of a lifetime. This does not necessarily mean spending your life's earnings, but the vacation should be special and should show your bride how much she means to you.

The honeymoon is traditionally your responsibility. However, you should get your fiancée involved in the planning of your honeymoon as it should be a joint decision as to where to go, how long to stay, and how much money to spend.

You will find many tools and suggestions on the following pages to help you plan this important trip. After reading this book, you will have information on different types of honeymoons, and you should be able to determine the perfect honeymoon destination for you and your bride, research and select a responsible travel agent, gather useful information using the resource leads provided, establish a reasonable budget with confidence, and - most importantly - walk away with the assurance that you are planning the honeymoon of a lifetime!

Start planning your honeymoon months before the wedding. Many locations that are popular with honeymooners tend to book fairly quickly, so the earlier you plan your trip, the better values you'll usually find.

There are many choices to make and many plans to be made but most of them seem to fall into place once you've made the toughest decision... where to go.

Many people have a preconceived notion of where a honeymoon should take place. And indeed, these locations are, year after year, some of the places most frequently visited by newlyweds. We'll take a look at some of these "traditional" destinations as well as some that are a little "less traditional."

Think about what you and your fiancée might find appealing (and unappealing) in the following honeymoon vacations. Be careful not to assume what your new bride may be looking for in a honeymoon. Couples are often surprised when they discover what the other partner considers a "vacation." Refer to the section entitled *Choosing A Destination* to determine what each other's ideal vacation includes.

*T*YPES OF

*H*ONEYMOONS

Listed on the following pages are sample honeymoon plans -- both traditional and less traditional. A brief description of some of the most popular honeymoon trips (ones that have remained popular with newlyweds for generations) is provided as well.

You can get very helpful information on planning a vacation package in the following brochures:

> United   States   Tour   Operator Association
> (212) 599-6599 www.ustoa.com
> - *How to Select a Tour Vacation Package*
> - *Worldwide Tour and Vacation Package Finder*
> - *The Standard for Confident Travel*

*T*RADITIONAL

*H*ONEYMOONS

• CRUISES

Cruises are a popular retreat for those who want the luxury of a hospitable resort with the added benefit of visiting one or more new areas. There are hundreds of different cruise options available to you. Typically, almost everything is included in the cost of your cruise: extravagant dining, unlimited group and individual activities, relaxing days and lively nights.

Costs vary greatly depending on the location the cruise will visit (if any) and your cabin accommodations. Locations range from traveling the Mississippi River to encircling the Greek Isles. Spend some time choosing your cabin. Most of them are small, but pay attention to distracting things, such as noisy areas and busy pathways, that might be located close by.

Even though most everything is included in your cost, be sure to ask about those items which may not be included. Request a helpful publication entitled *Answers to Your Most Frequently Asked Questions*, published by Cruise Lines International Association, (212) 921-0066, www.cruising.org.

• ALL INCLUSIVE RESORTS

Many newlyweds, tired from the previous months of wedding planning and accompanying stress, opt for the worry-free guarantee of an all-inclusive resort. Some resorts are for the entire family, some are for couples only (not necessarily newlywed), and some are strictly for honeymooners. Most of these resorts are nestled on a picturesque island beach catering to your relaxation needs.

Most offer numerous sports, water activities, entertainment, and exceptional service and attention. Your costs will vary depending on the location you choose, and there are many, many to choose from. "All-inclusive" means everything is included in your price. You won't have to worry about meals, drinks, tour fees or even tips.

One way of considering if this is a good option for you is to list all of the activities that the vacation package offers that you are interested in. Add up the individual costs and compare. If you wouldn't be participating much in the activities, food, and drink, you may actually save money by arranging your own trip at an independent resort. Even still, many couples prefer to spend the extra money in exchange for a vacation free of planning and wearying decisions.

Because of its convenience, many couples choose this resort option as the setting for their honeymoon. Some of the most popular all-inclusive resorts are Club Med and Sandals.

• THE POCONOS

The Poconos Honeymoon resorts are located in Pennsylvania and are considered to be some of the most popular Honeymoon destinations around. The Poconos offer a variety of individual resorts, each heavily laden with fanciful symbols of romance and sweet desires. The atmosphere is perfect for those who want to be enveloped in a surrounding where you'll never forget you're in love and on your honeymoon. Some travel packages here are considered all-inclusive, but as always, be sure to ask about exclusions and extras.

Poconos tourism information:
1-800-POCONOS   www.800poconos.com

• WALT DISNEY WORLD

Another popular destination for those seeking a "theme" resort are those offered as *Disney's Fairy Tale Honeymoons*.   These vacation packages include accommodations at Disney's exclusive resorts and admission to their theme parks.   Some packages are also available with accommodations at some of the privately owned resorts at Disney World.   Prices for Disney packages can range greatly depending on your tastes and the amount of activity you desire. For information about Disney's honeymoon packages, call (407) 828-3400 or visit online at www.disneyweddings.com.

Inquire with your travel agent about day or overnight cruises leaving from nearby ports in Florida. This is one way to combine two very popular honeymoon options into one!

Other popular and traditional honeymoon plans are as follows:

- Enjoying the beaches and unique treasures of the Hawaiian islands

- Exploring Northern California's romantic wine country

- Ski and snowboard package getaways in Vermont, New Hampshire, Colorado, and Northern California

- Camping and hiking within the beautiful and adventurous National Parks

- Sightseeing, touring, and exploring a variety of points in Europe via the rail system

- Island hopping on a cruise ship around the Greek Isles

- Enjoying a fanciful and adventurous journey on the Orient Express

*L*ESS

*T*RADITIONAL

*H*ONEYMOONS

- Bicycling in Nova Scotia while relaxing at quaint Bed and Breakfast Inns

- Participating in a white water river rafting expedition in Oregon

- Mingling with the owners and fellow guests on an Old West Dude Ranch

- Visiting landmarks and parks while enjoying the convenience of a traveling home in a rented RV

- Mustering up the courage and stamina for an aggressive hiking tour of the Canadian Rockies

- Training for and participating in a dog sled race in the brisk tundra of Alaska

- "Roughing it" while enjoying the splendor of a safari in East Africa

CHOOSING YOUR DESTINATION

Maybe your idea of a perfect honeymoon is 10 days of adventure and discovery; but for your fiancée, it may be 10 days of resting in a beach chair and romantic strolls in the evening. The choices for honeymoon vacations are as varied as the bride and groom themselves. Deciding together on a honeymoon destination is a wonderful opportunity to discover more about each other and negotiate a vacation that will leave both of you relaxed, fulfilled, and even more in love.

First, determine the type of atmosphere and climate you prefer. Then consider the types of activities you would like to engage in.

Do you want the weather to be hot for swimming at the beach... or warm for long guided tours of unknown cities... or cooler for day-long hikes in the woods... or cold for optimum skiing conditions? Keep in mind the time of year in which your wedding falls. Will you be escaping from warm or cool temperatures?

If you have a specific destination in mind, you (or your travel agent) will need to do some research to be sure the weather conditions will be suitable for your planned activities.

Review the previous chapters on traditional and non-traditional honeymoons and note what you feel are the pros and cons of each type of vacation. The two of you should have lots of images and possibilities in your mind at this point! The next step is to determine the most perfect atmosphere to provide the setting for your honeymoon. The following sections, *Creating A Wish List* and *Helpful Resources*, will guide you through this next step and beyond.

CREATING A

WISH LIST

Together with your fiancée, complete the following wish list worksheet. You should each check off your preferences even if both of you don't agree on them. There are many locations that provide a variety of activities. Remember, you don't need to spend every minute of your honeymoon together, but your honeymoon destination should be one that intrigues both of you.

This worksheet is divided into 5 sections. You will be considering location, accommodations, meals, activities, and night life.

While responding to the following, be as true to your interests as possible; don't concern yourself with finances and practicality at this point. This is your chance to let your mind wander! Think about what you would like to fill your days and nights with. This is the honeymoon of your dreams...

You step out of the plane, train, car or boat that took you to your honeymoon destination. You sigh with satisfaction at the memory of your flawless and enjoyable wedding as your feet touch the ground.

What type of overall atmosphere do you see yourself stepping into?

What is the weather like?

Do you picture a long stretch of beach, towering mountains, blossoming vineyards, or city skyscrapers? Is the dry sand of the desert blowing around or is everything captured under glistening snowcaps?

Are there many people walking around (many locals, many tourists), or is it a secluded retreat?

Are you relaxing indoors in a resort with a pampering environment that caters to your comfort? Do you return to a simple, modest hotel or motel after a long day of sightseeing, touring, and dining? Are you camping in the middle of your activities --hiking, climbing, fishing, etc.?

Do you see yourself interacting much with others? Would you like to have these activities be organized? Are there vistas and horizons to gaze endlessly upon, or is there an abundance of visual activity and changing scenery?

Are you enjoying exotic foods elaborately displayed and available to you at your leisure? Are you testing out your sense of adventure on the local cuisine and dining hot spots? Are you eating fast foods and pizza in exchange for spending your time and money on other items and activities that make your vacation exciting?

Are your evenings filled with romantic strolls or festivities that run late into the night? Are you staying in for romantic evenings or re-energizing for another busy day of honeymooning?

HOW TO USE THIS WORKSHEET:

Each of you separately should place a check mark next to the items or images on the wish list that appeal to you. After you have finished, highlight those items that both of you feel are important (the items that were checked by both of you).

Then each of you should highlight, in a different colored marker or pen, 2-3 items in each category that you feel are very important to you (even though the other person may not have checked it off.)

$\mathcal{B}$ = *BRIDE* $\mathcal{G}$ = *GROOM*	$\mathcal{B}$ ✓	$\mathcal{G}$ ✓
Location:		
hot weather		
mild weather		
cold weather		
dry climate		
moist climate		
sand and beaches		
lakes/ponds		
wilderness/wooded areas		
mountains		
fields		
city streets		
small local town		
large metropolitan area		
popular tourist destination		
visiting among the locals		
nighttime weather conducive to outdoor activities		
nighttime weather conducive to indoor activities		

$\mathscr{B}$ = BRIDE $\mathscr{G}$ = GROOM	$\mathscr{B}$ ✓	$\mathscr{G}$ ✓
"modern" resources and service available		
"roughing it" on your own		
culture and customs you are familiar and comfortable with		
new cultures and customs you would like to get to know		
Accommodations:		
part of a larger resort community		
a stand alone building		
lodging amongst other fellow tourists		
lodging amongst couples only		
lodging amongst fellow newlyweds only		
lodging amongst locals		
large room or suite		
plush, highly decorated surroundings		

$\mathcal{B}$ = **BRIDE** $\mathcal{G}$ = **GROOM**	$\mathcal{B}$ ✓	$\mathcal{G}$ ✓
modestly sized room		
modest decor		
balcony		
private Jacuzzi in room		
room service		
chamber maid service		
laundry service available		
laundry room available		
beauty salon on premises		
workout gym on premises		
gift shop on premises		
pool on premises		
poolside bar service		
sauna, hot tub on premises		
common gathering lounge for guests		

$\mathcal{B}$ = BRIDE $\mathcal{G}$ = GROOM	$\mathcal{B}$ ✓	$\mathcal{G}$ ✓
Meals:		
casual dining		
formal dining		
prepared by executive chefs		
prepared by yourself/grocery store		
variety of local and regional restaurants		
traditional "American" cuisine		
opportunity for picnics		
exotic, international menu		
formal dining		
entertainment while dining		
planned meal times		
dining based on your own schedule		
fast food restaurants		
vegetarian meals		
special diet meals		
delis		

B = BRIDE *G = GROOM*	*B* ✓	*G* ✓
diners		
Activities:		
sun bathing		
snorkeling		
diving		
swimming		
jet skiing		
water skiing		
fishing		
sailing		
snow skiing		
snow boarding		
hiking		
camping		
rock climbing		
golf		
tennis		
aerobics		

B = **BRIDE** *G* = **GROOM**	*B* ✓	*G* ✓
site-seeing suggestions and guidance		
planned bus/guided tours		
ability to go off on your own		
historic tours		
art museums		
theater		
exploring family heritage		
Night Life:		
quiet strolls		
outdoor activities		
sitting and relaxing outdoors		
sitting and relaxing in front of a fireplace		
being alone with each other		
being out with the locals		
being out with other newlyweds		

$\mathscr{B}$ = **BRIDE** $\mathscr{G}$ = **GROOM**	$\mathscr{B}$ ✓	$\mathscr{G}$ ✓
discovering new cultures and forms of entertainment		
dancing		
visiting bars/pubs		
theater/shows		
gambling		
Other important elements:		

Your wish lists, at this point, probably look like a list of *all* of the positive elements of *all* of your dream vacations combined. List as many things as you can think of. The more information you have, the better the suggestions your travel agent (or yourself if you'll be doing your own research) will be able to make.

Together, using this wish list, you will discover a honeymoon destination and match a honeymoon style that will fulfill your dreams.

The resource leads and exercises provided in the rest of this book will help you get from wish list to reality. Happy planning!

PERSONAL

NOTES

*H*ELPFUL

*R*ESOURCES

Now that you have a completed wish list, take this list to your travel agent. If you don't already have a travel agent, use the following section for help in selecting a reputable agent.

A good travel agent, especially one who works with a lot of honeymooners, will be able to tell you about several different places that match your wish list while staying within your budget. (The section entitled *Creating A Budget* will prove invaluable in determining exactly what your budget will be). Your travel agent should be able to provide a variety of options which contain different combinations of the elements of your wish list. Discuss with him/her which "lower priority" items you are willing to forego in order to experience the best of your "top priorities."

TRAVEL AGENTS

Hiring the services of a good travel agent will take a lot of unnecessary pressure off of you. In the past, you may have felt that you did not need the assistance of a travel agent when planning a vacation. Planning a honeymoon, however, can often be far more involved and stressful than a "regular" vacation, due to the simple fact that you are also deeply enmeshed in the planning of your wedding!

Therefore, you should take advantage of the professional resources available to you when working out the small details and finding the best values. Keep in mind, though, that you will still probably want to do some research on your own, ask for second opinions, and, most of all, read the fine print.

Since a travel agent can become one of your most valuable resources, you will want to consider a few important things when trying to select one:

Ask family, friends, and coworkers for personal recommendations (especially from former honeymooners).

If you are unable to find an agent through a personal referral, then select a few agencies that are established nearby (from newspapers, phone books, etc.)

Next, you will want to make an appointment with an agent or speak to one over the phone. Pay close attention to the following and then make your decision.

Find out if they are a member of the *American Society of Travel Agents* (ASTA). Additionally, find out if they are also a *Certified Travel Counselor* (CTC), or possibly a *Destination Specialist* (DS).

ASTA: Members of this organization are required to have at least 5 years travel agent experience.   They also agree to adhere to strict codes and standards of integrity in travel issues as established by the national society. In most states, there are no formal regulations requiring certain qualifications for being a travel agent. In other words, any person can decide to call him/herself, and thus advertise as, a travel agent.

CTC: Certified Travel Counselors have successfully completed a 2 year program in travel management.

DS: Destination Specialists have successfully completed studies focusing on a particular region.

For a list of ASTA agencies in your area, call or write:

American Society of Travel Agents
Consumer Affairs Department
1101 King Street, Suite 200
Alexandria, VA 22314
(703) 739-2782
www.ASTAnet.com

A listing for the local chapter in your area can also be found in your local phone book or visit their web site at **www.astanet.com**.

For a list of Destination Specialists and Certified Travel Agents in your area, call or write:

Institute of Certified Travel Agents
148 Linden Street
P.O. Box 56
Wellesley, MA 02181
(800) 542-4282
(press "0" to be connected to a Travel Counselor)
www.ICTA.com

Questions to Qualify Your Travel Agent

How long has the Travel Agency been in business?

How long has the Travel Agent been with the agency?

How much experience does the Travel Agent have? Any special studies or travels?

Do they have a good resource library?

Does the agent/agency have a variety of brochures to offer?

Do they have video tapes to lend?

Do they have a recommended reading list of travel aid books?

Does the agent seem to understand your responses on your wish list and budget?

Does he/she seem excited to help you?

Does the agent listen carefully to your ideas? Take notes on your conversations? Ask you questions to ensure a full understanding?

Is the agent able to offer a variety of different possibilities that suit your interests based on your wish list? Do the suggestions fall within your budget?

Can the agent relay back to you (in his/her own words) what your wish list priorities are? What your budget priorities are?

Is the agent prompt in getting back in touch with you?

Is the agent reasonably quick in coming up with suggestions and alternatives? Are the suggestions exciting and within reason?

Does the agent take notes on your interests (degree of sports, leisure, food, etc.)?

Does the travel agency provide a 24 hour emergency help line?

Are you documenting your conversations and getting all of your travel plans and reservations confirmed in writing?

Aside from just offering information and arrangements about locations and discounts, a good travel agent should also provide you with information about passports, customs, travel and health insurance, travelers' checks, and any other information important to a traveler.

OTHER SOURCES

National bridal magazines and general travel magazines are a great place to search for honeymoon ideas. But remember, you cannot always believe every word in paid advertising.

In addition to the information your travel agent provides, you can also attain maps, brochures, and other useful items on your own. At the end of this section, you will find many useful phone numbers to help you in contacting tourist bureaus and travel agencies worldwide. These offices are extremely helpful in acquiring both general information (information about the weather, tourist attractions, landmarks, and even coupons or promotional brochures "selling" the area) and more specific information about reputable hotels, inns, bed and breakfasts, restaurants, etc.

Also provided in this section are phone numbers for sources specializing in information about traveling by train (in the United States as well as abroad) and for camping and hiking throughout the country.

Your local library, the travel section of book stores, and travel stores are also excellent sources for finding information and tips relevant to your travel needs. You will find books on traveling in general as well as books specific to the region or destination you will be visiting. There are numerous tour books, maps, language books and tapes, as well as books about a location's culture, traditions, customs, climate, and geography.

These books are a great source of information since they are independent from the locations they describe and are therefore impartial, objective, and usually contain correct, unbiased information. You can also find books and other resources describing (and sometimes rating) restaurants, hotels, shows, and tours. Books on bargain hunting and finding the best deals are common as well.

SOURCES TO READ

The Traveler's Reading Guide: Ready-Made Reading Lists for the Armchair Traveler, by Maggy Simone
> *A comprehensive listing of varied travel resources for almost every place in the world.*

The Stephen Birnbaum Travel Guides

Frommer's Guides

Michelin's Green Guides

Michelin's Red Guides

Insight Guides

Let's Go! guides

Fodor's Guides

Fielding Travel Books

AYH Handbook and Hosteler's Manual: Europe

AYH Handbook and Hosteler's Manual: United States

The New York Times Practical Traveler

Mobil Travel Guide

Background Notes

U.S. Government notes containing information about the culture, people, geography, history, government, economy, and maps of most countries worldwide.

The U.S. Government Printing Office
Cost: $1.00
(1-202-512-1800)
or download at: www.access.gpo.gov

101 Tips For Adventure Travelers

Overseas Adventure Travel
(1-800-221-0814)
www.overseasadventuretravel.com

National Park Service publications:

(1-202-208-4747) www.nps.gov
* *National Park System Map and Guide*
* *The National Parks: Index*

National Forest Service publications:

(1-202-205-8333) www.fs.fed.us
A Guide to Your National Forests

The Internet

If you have Internet access you can acquire volumes and volumes of information (and titillating pictures) about your destination or even "chat" with other soon-to-be honeymooners. If you don't currently have access, local   libraries often provide limited free time and user-assistance for their members.

SOURCES TO CALL

State Tourism Bureaus

Alabama Bureau of Tourism
800-ALABAMA, www.touralabama.com
Alaska Travel Industry Association
907-929-2200, www.travelalaska.com
Arizona Office of Tourism
800-842-8257, www.arizonaguide.com
Arkansas Dept. of Parks and Tourism
800-828-8974, www.arkansas.com
California Tourism Office
800-862-2543, www.gocalif.com
Colorado Tourism Board
800-COLORADO, www.colorado.com
Connecticut Vacation Center
800-CT-BOUND, www.ctbound.com
D.C. Convention and Visitors Association
202-789-7000, www.washington.org
Delaware Tourism Office
800-441-8846, www.visitdelaware.net
Florida Tourist Bureau
800-304-9381, www.floridatouristbureau.com
Georgia Department of Industry & Trade
800-VISIT-GA, www.georgia.org
Hawaii Bureau of Tourism
800-303-2408I, www.hawaii.com
Idaho Division of Tourism Development
800-635-7820, www.visitid.org
Illinois Bureau of Tourism
800-226-6632, www.enjoyillinois.com

Indiana Department of Commerce
800-289-6646, www.enjoyindiana.com
Iowa Office of Tourism
800-345-IOWA, www.traveliowa.com
Kansas Department of Travel & Tourism
800-2-KANSAS, www.travelks.com
Kentucky Dept. of Travel Development
800-225-TRIP, www.kentuckytourism.com
Louisiana Office of Tourism
800-33-GUMBO, www.louisianatravel.com
Maine Bureau of Tourism
888-624-6345, www.visitmaine.com
Maryland Office of Tourist Development
800-543-1036, www.mdisfun.org
Massachusetts Department of Tourism
800-447-MASS, www.massvacation.com
Michigan Department of Commerce
888-78-GREAT, www.michigan.org
Minnesota Office of Tourism
800-657-3700, www.exploreminnesota.com
Mississippi Office of Tourism
800-WARMEST, www.visitmississippi.org
Missouri Division of Tourism
800-877-1234, www.missouritourism.org
Montana Travel Promotion Division
800-VISIT-MT, www.visitmt.com
Nebraska Dept. of Travel and Tourism
800-228-4307, www.visitnebraska.org
Nevada Commission on Tourism
800-NEVADA-8, www.travelnevada.com
New Hampshire Division of Tourism
800-FUN-IN-NH, www.visitnh.gov

New Jersey Office of Travel & Tourism
800-JERSEY-7, www.visitnj.org
New Mexico Dept. of Tourism
800-SEE-NEWMEX, www.newmexico.org
New York Division of Tourism
New York State: 800-CALL-NYS
www.iloveny.com
North Carolina Travel & Tourism Div.
800-VISIT-NC, www.visitnc.com
North Dakota Tourism Division
800-HELLO-ND, www.ndtourism.com
Ohio Department of Travel & Tourism
800-BUCKEYE, www.ohiotourism.com
Oklahoma Tourism and Recreation Dept.
800-652-6552, www.travelok.com
Oregon Tourism Commission
800-547-7842, www.traveloregon.com
Pennsylvania Department of Tourism
800-VISIT-PA, www.state.pa.us/visit/
 800-POCONOS, www.800poconos.com
Rhode Island Tourism Division
800-556-2484, www.visitrhodeisland.com
**South Carolina Department of Parks,
        Recreation, and Tourism**
800-346-3634, www.travelsc.com
South Dakota Division of Tourism
800-S-DAKOTA, www.travelsd.com
Tennessee Department of Tourism
800-GO-2TENN, www.tourism.state.tn.us/
Texas Travel and Information Bureau
800-888-8-TEX, www.traveltex.com
Utah Travel Council
800-200-1160, www.utah.com

Vermont Travel Division
800-VERMONT, www.travel-vermont.com
Virginia Division of Tourism
800-VISIT-VA, www.virginia.org
Washington Tourism Development
800-544-1800,
www.experiencewashington.com
West Virginia Div. of Tourism & Parks
800-CALL-WVA, www.callwva.com
Wisconsin Division of Tourism
800-432-TRIP, www.travelwisconsin.com
Wyoming Division of Tourism
800-CALL-WYO,
www.wyomingtourism.org
U.S. Virgin Islands Division of Tourism
800-372-USVI, www.USVI.org

International Tourism Bureaus

Anguilla Tourist Information
800-553-4939, www.anguilla-vacation.com
Antigua Tourist Office
212-541-4117, www.antigua-barbuda.org
Argentina Tourist Information
800-722-5737, www.wam.com/ar/tourism
Aruba Tourism Authority
404-89-ARUBA, www.aruba.com
Australian Tourist Commission
800-445-4400, www.australia.com
Austrian National Tourist Office
310-477-2038, www.experienceaustria.com
Bahamas Tourist Office
800-422-4262, www.bahamas.com

Balkan Holidays
800-822-1106, www.balkantourist.net
Barbados Board of Tourism
800-221-9831, www.barbados.org
Belgian Tourist Office
212-355-7675, www.belgium-tourism.com
Belize Tourist Board
800-624-0686, www.travelbelize.org
Bermuda Department of Tourism
800-223-6106, www.bermudatourism.com
Bonaire Tourist Information Office
800-BONAIRE, www.infobonaire.com
Brazil Tourism Office
800-544-5503, www.brazilres.com
British Tourist Office
800-462-2748, www.travelbritain.org
Canadian Consulate
613-946-1000, www.travelcanada.ca
Alberta: 800-661-8888
BritishColumbia: 800-HELLO-BC
Manitoba: 800-665-0040
New Brunswick: 800-561-0123
Newfoundland: 800-563-6353
NovaScotia: 800-565-0000
Ontario: 800-ONTARIO
PrinceEdward: 800-PEI-PLAY
Quebec: 877-BON-JOUR
Saskatchewan: 877-2-ESCAPE
Yukon: 867-667-5340
Caribbean Tourism Organization
800-603-3545, www.caribtourism.com
Cayman Islands Department of Tourism
213-738-1968, www.caymanislands.ky

Chile National Tourist Board
800-244-5366, www.visitchile.org
China National Tourist Office
818-545-7505, www.cnto.org
Colombian Consulate
202-332-7476, www.colombiaemb.org
Cook Islands Tourist Authority
888-994-2665, www.cook-islands.com
Costa Rican Tourist Board
800-343-6332, www.tourism-costarica.com
Curacao Tourist Board
800-270-3350, www.curacao-tourism.com
Cyprus Consulate General
212-683-5280, www.cyprustourism.org
CEDOK (Czech Republic and Slovakia)
212-288-0830, www.czechcenter.com
Denmark Tourist Board
212-885-9700, www.visitdenmark.com
Dominican Republic Tourist Info. Center
888-DR-INFO, www.dominica.com
Egyptian Tourist Authority
877-773-4978, http://touregypt.net
Fiji Visitors Bureau
800-YEA-FIJI, www.BulaFiji.com
Finland Tourist Board
800-FIN-INFO, www.mek.fi/us
French Government Tourist Office
310-271-6665, www.francetourism.com
French West Indies (St. Martin,
            Martinique, Guadeloupe)
877-956-1234, www.franceguide.com
German National Tourist Office
310-234-0250, www.us.germany-tourism.de

Greece National Tourist Authority
212-421-5777, www.gnto.gr
Grenada Department of Tourism
212-687-9554, www.grenada.org
Guam Visitors Bureau
800-US3-GUAM, www.visitguam.org
Guatemala Tourist Commission
202-745-3873, www.inguat.net
Honduras Tourist Bureau
800-410-9608, www.honduras.com
Hong Kong Tourist Association
212-421-3382, www.hkta.org/usa
Hungary Tourist Board
212-355-0240, www.hungarytourism.com
Iceland Tourist Board
212-885-9747, www.icetourist.is
India Tourist Office
800-953-9399, www.tourisminindia.com
Indonesian Tourist Office
866-INDONESIA,
www.indonesia-tourism.com
Ireland Tourist Board
800-223-6470, www.ireland.travel.ie
Israeli Government Tourist Office
888-77-ISRAEL, www.goisrael.com
Italian Tourist Office
310-820-0098, www.italiantourism.com
Jamaican Tourist Board
800-JAMAICA, www.jamaicatravel.com
Japan National Tourist Office
212-757-5640, www.jnto.go.jp
Kenya Tourist Office
212-486-1300, www.kenyatourism.org

Korea National Tourist Office
800-868-7567, www.visitkorea.or.kr
Luxembourg National Tourist Office
212-935-8888, www.etat.lu/tourism
Macau Tourist Office
853-315-5660 www.macautourism.gov.mo
Malaysian Tourist Centre
213-689-9702, www.visitmalaysia.com
Malta National Tourist Office
887-GO-MALTA, www.visitmalta.com
Mexican Tourist Office
800-44-MEXICO, www.mexico-travel.com
Monaco Government Tourist Office
800-753-9696, www.monaco-congres.com
Morocco National Tourist Office
407-827-5337,
www.tourism-in-morocco.com
Netherlands Board of Tourism
888-GO-HOLLAND, www.goholland.com
New Zealand Tourist Office
800-388-5494, www.tourisminfo.govt.nz
Norway Scandinavia Tourist Offices
212-421-7333, www.norway.org
Panama Tourist Bureau
507-226-7000, www.ipat.gob.pa
Papua/New Guinea Tourist Office
949-752-5440, www.paradiselives.org.pg
Philippine Department of Tourism
213-487-4525, www.tourism.gov.ph
Poland National Tourism Office
212-338-9412, www.polandtour.org
Portugal National Tourist Office
212-354-4403, www.portugal.org

Puerto Rico Tourism Office
800-866-STAR, www.prtourism.com
Romanian National Tourist Office
212-545-8484, www.romaniatravel.com
Russian Travel Information Office
877-221-7120, www.russia-travel.com
Singapore Tourist Board
323-852-1901, www.singapore-usa.com
South African Tourism Board
800-822-5368, www.satour.org
Spain National Tourism Office
212-265-8822, www.okspain.org
Sri Lanka Tourist Board
202-483-4025, www.lanka.net/ctb
St. Kitts Tourist Board
212-535-1234, www. stkitts-nevis.com
St. Lucia Tourist Board
800-4-STLUCIA, www.stlucia.org
St. Maarten Tourist Office
800-786-2278, www.st-maarteen.com
St. Vincent/Grenadines Tourist Office
800-235-3029, www.svgtourism.com
Sweden Travel & Tourism Board
212-885-9700, www.gosweden.org
Switzerland National Tourist Office
800-SWISS, www.myswitzerland.com
Tahitian Tourist Board
877-697-6019, www.tahiti-tourisme.com
Taiwan Visitors Association
212-867-1632, www.tbroc.gov.tw
Thailand Tourism Authority
212-432-0433, www.tourismthailand.org

Trinidad and Tobago Tourist Board
888-595-4TNT, www.visitTNT.com
Tunisian Tourist Office
202-862-1850, www.tunisiaonline.com
Turkish Tourism Office
212-687-2194, www.tourismturkey.org
Venezuela Tourism Association
415-331-0100, www.venezuela.com

Other

National Park Service
Office of Public Inquiries
202-208-4747
American Automobile Association
Travel Related Services
Department
407-444-8000
Amtrak National Railroad Passenger Information
800-872-7245
Rail Europe
800-438-7245
Via Rail Canada
800-561-3949

CREATING A

BUDGET

You want your honeymoon to give you luxurious experiences and priceless memories. But you don't want to return from your vacation to be faced with debts and unnecessary feelings of guilt for not having stayed within a reasonable budget.

This should be the vacation of a lifetime. You can make this trip into anything your imagination allows. Pay attention to which experiences or details you would consider a "must have" and prioritize. As you work with your budget, stay focused on those top priority items and allow less "elaborate" solutions for lower priority items. If you stay true to your most important vacation objectives, the minor sacrifices along the way will barely be noticed.

Perhaps, at this point, you don't know how many days your honeymoon will last.

Often, the number of days you'll vacation depends on the type of honeymoon you choose. If you (and your travel agent) are designing your own honeymoon, the typical cost-per-day will most likely determine your length of stay. If you opt for a cruise or another type of prearranged vacation, your length of stay will probably be dependent upon the designated length of the travel package. By determining a basic, overall budget at the start, you will know what your limits are.

Yes, this is a very romantic time... but try to remain realistic! Once you have an idea of your spending limits, your choices will be much easier to make.

Don't be discouraged if you're unable to spend an infinite amount of money on this trip. Very few couples are able to live life so carefree. You can still experience a honeymoon that will leave you filled with those priceless memories... it's all in the planning!

The following budget worksheets will help guide you in creating your honeymoon budget. You may want to make copies of this worksheet so that you can create several budget plans. Keep trying different variations until you are satisfied with how your expenses will be allocated. When comparing your potential honeymoon options, you'll find that laying out a simple budget is an effective, and essential, tool for making decisions.

GENERAL BUDGET

Traditionally the groom is responsible for the honeymoon. The groom will take on the challenges of gathering information and working through the necessary details of providing a perfect honeymoon for his new bride... and himself! Nowadays, many couples find it necessary for both the bride and groom to contribute to the cost in order to experience the honeymoon of their dreams. (*Today, the average newlywed couple spends $2,500-$3,500 on their honeymoon.*) Many couples, together, determine what each partner will contribute and then shape the budget from there.

Some couples find that including the suggestion of a "Money Contribution towards a Memorable Honeymoon" as a gift in their bridal registry is a great way for friends and family to contribute to the trip. Some couples also include some version of a "Dollar Dance" at their reception. This is a great way for the bride and groom to dance with many of their guests while accepting the dollar "dance fee" as a contribution to their honeymoon. Some couples choose to pursue less romantic options for building up the honeymoon savings... part time jobs, yard sales, etc..

Whatever your methods may be, remember that increasing the amount of money you will spend does not automatically ensure a more pleasurable and enjoyable vacation. Your most important and effective resource is your commitment to planning. You will see that, regardless of what your budget limits may be, your vacation possibilities are endless.

Note: Even if you think you have a good sense of what you will spend (or even if you plan on going with an all-inclusive package) going through this exercise is a smart way to ensure that there will be no surprises later on.

OVERALL BUDGET:

Amount from Wedding Budget set aside for Honeymoon:

$_____

Amount Groom is able to contribute from current funds/savings:

$_____

Amount Bride is able to contribute from current funds/savings:

$_____

Amount to be saved/acquired by Groom from now until the honeymoon date:
(monthly contributions, part-time job, gifts, bonuses)

$_____

Amount to be saved/acquired by Bride from now until the honeymoon date:
(monthly contributions, part-time job, gifts, bonuses)

$_____

OVERALL BUDGET AMOUNT:

$_____

Budget Notes

DETAILED BUDGET

BEFORE THE HONEYMOON:

Special honeymoon clothing purchases:

$_____

Bride's trousseau (honeymoon lingerie):

$_____

Sundries:

>(HELPFUL HINT: Make a list of what you already have and what you need to purchase. You can then use these lists as part of your Packing List. See *Packing Checklist.*)

$_____

Film, disposable cameras, extra camera batteries:

$_____

Maps, guide books, travel magazines:

$_____

Foreign language books and tapes, translation dictionary:

$_____

Passport photos, application fees:
(See *International Travel)*

$_____

Medical exam, inoculations:
> (See *International Travel*)

$_____

New blank journal:
> (IDEA: Create a beautiful *Honeymoon Memory Book* with a simple blank journal. Fill this journal with your thoughts, record of activities, mementos, phone numbers from new acquaintances, and travel notes from your honeymoon to enjoy and reminisce whenever you need an escape.)

$_____

Other items: _____

_____

$_____

BEFORE THE HONEYMOON
TOTAL AMOUNT:

$_____

DURING THE HONEYMOON:

TRANSPORTATION
Airplane tickets:

$_____

Shuttle or cab (to and from airport):

$_____

Car rental :

$_____

Gasoline, tolls:

$_____

Taxis, buses, other public transportation:

$_____

Tips:

$_____

TRANSPORTATION
TOTAL AMOUNT:

$_____

ACCOMMODATIONS

Hotel/resort room (total for entire stay):

$ _____

Room service:

$ _____

Miscellaneous "hidden costs":

> Phone use, room taxes and surcharges, chambermaid and room service tips (see *Tipping Guide*), in-room liquor bar and snacks.

$ _____

**ACCOMMODATIONS
TOTAL AMOUNT:**

$ _____

MEALS

(NOTE: Don't forget to include the cost of drinks and gratuities in your meal estimates.)

Breakfast: $_____ *per meal*

x _____ # *days* = $_____

Lunch: $_____ *per meal*

x _____ # *days* = $_____

Casual Dinners: $_____ *per meal*

x _____ # *days* = $_____

Formal Dinners: $_____ *per meal*

x _____ # *days* = $_____

**Picnics, Snacks,
Temptations:** $_____ *per day*

x _____ # *days* = $_____

MEALS
TOTAL AMOUNT:

$_____

ENTERTAINMENT

Sport and activity lessons (tennis, golf, ballroom dancing, etc.):

$_____

Day excursions and tours (boat tours, diving, snorkeling, bus/guided tours, etc.):

$_____

Shows, theater:

$_____

Lounges, nightclubs, discos:
(don't forget to include the cost of drinks and bar gratuities)

$_____

Museum fees:

$_____

Pampering (massages, spa treatments, hairdresser, etc.):

$_____

ENTERTAINMENT
TOTAL AMOUNT:

$_____

MISCELLANEOUS

Souvenirs for yourselves:

$_____

Souvenirs and gifts for family and friends:

$_____

Postcards (including cost of stamps):

$_____

Newspapers and magazines:

$_____

Additional film, replacement sundries, other:

$_____

MISCELLANEOUS
TOTAL AMOUNT:

$_____

AFTER THE HONEYMOON:

Film developing costs:

$\underline{\hspace{6cm}}$

Photo Albums:

$\underline{\hspace{6cm}}$

> ### *AFTER THE HONEYMOON* TOTAL AMOUNT:
>
> $\underline{\hspace{5cm}}$

For All-Inclusive Resorts/Cruises and Travel Packages only:

Fill in the entire budget form above (simply put a "$0.00" on items to be included in the total package price), then list the total inclusive package price on the line below. Don't forget to include taxes and surcharges.

Inclusive Package Price:

$\underline{\hspace{6cm}}$

SPECIFIC BUDGET AMOUNT:

$ _____

Doing a budget analysis may be one of the most useful things you can do in planning your honeymoon. With all the options available, a good cost analysis will help make the most appropriate decisions very clear to you.

First, create a budget using the above work-sheet for what you think allows for an ideal, yet reasonable, honeymoon. Highlight those expenses which are top priorities. For example, a spacious, ritzy hotel room may be the most important element for you. Or perhaps participating in numerous sports activities and excursions or enjoying fine dining is more important than a spacious room.

Next, as you come across different destina-tions and options that appeal to you, fill in a new budget worksheet. Compare the results to other potential trips. See how your prior-ity items on each trip compare to one an-other. Determine the pros and cons of each.

This is also an effective way of looking at the pros and cons of an all-inclusive package versus an independently organized trip.

NOTE: Once you've decided on your honeymoon destination and activities, fill in a new budget as accurately as possible and take it with you on your trip. Use it to chart your expenses as they occur so you will have a visual guide of whether or not you are staying within budget.

If you find that you are going over your budget, take a look at those top priority items that you'd still like to keep. See if you can eliminate some lower priority items to free up some money for the favored ones.

If you find you are under budget, celebrate with a special "gift" for yourselves (massages, an extravagant dinner, another afternoon of jet skiing, etc.).

TIPPING GUIDE

This guide is provided to help you get familiar with customary gratuity standards you may encounter throughout your travels.

Tipping customs vary from country to country. It is advisable to inquire about tipping with the international tourism board representing the country you'll be traveling in. Simply ask for information about tipping customs and social expectations. You will also want to discuss gratuities with your travel agent or planner. Some travel packages include gratuities in the total cost, some leave that to the guests, and some even discourage tipping (usually because they have built it into the total package price) Be sure to discuss this with your travel planner.

SERVICE	GRATUITY
AIR TRAVEL	
Skycaps	$1.00 per bag
Flight Attendants	none
ROAD TRAVEL	
Taxi Drivers	15% of fare (no less than 50 cents)
Limousine Driver	usually included in bill
Valet Parking	$1.00
Tour Bus Guide	$1.00
RAIL TRAVEL	
Redcaps	$1.00 per bag (or posted rate plus 50 cents)
Sleeping Car Attendant	$1.00 per person
Train Conductor and Crew	none
Dining Car Attendant	15% of bill

CRUISE	
Cabin Steward	2.5-7.5% of fare (paid at the end of the trip)
Dining Room Waiter	2.5-7.5% of fare (paid at the end of the trip)
Cabin Boy, Bar Steward, Wine Steward	5-7.5% of total fare (divided proportionately among them)
RESTAURANTS	
Maitre d', Headwaiter	none (unless special services provided, then typically $5.00)
Waiter/Waitress	15% of bill (pretax total)
Bartender	15% of bill
Wine Steward	15% of bill
Washroom Attendant	25-50 cents
Coat Check Attendant	$1.00 for 1 or 2 coats
(NOTE: Some restaurants in foreign countries add the gratuity and/or service charge to your bill. If it has not been added, tip the customary regional rate.)	

HOTEL / RESORT	
Concierge	$2.00-10.00 for special attention or arrangements
Doorman	$1.00 for hailing taxi
Bellhop	$1.00 per bag 50 cents for showing room
Room Service	15% of bill
Chamber Maid	$1.00-2.00 per day or $5.00-10.00 per week for longer stays (no tip for one night stays)
Pool Attendant	50 cents for towel service
MISCELLANEOUS	
Barbershop	15% of cost
Beauty Salon	15% of cost
Manicure	$1.00-5.00 depending on cost of service
Facial	15% of cost
Massage	15% of cost

THINGS TO PACK

TRAVELERS' FIRST AID KIT:

Consider the differences in the climates of where you live now and where you'll be visiting. Also consider the air conditions of airplanes, trains and boats. Bring along items that will help in the transition and keep you feeling as comfortable as possible.

- ☐ *Aspirin*
- ☐ *Antacid tablets*
- ☐ *Diarrhea medication*
- ☐ *Cold remedies/ sinus decongestant*
- ☐ *Throat lozenges*
- ☐ *Antiseptic Lotion*
- ☐ *Band-Aids*
- ☐ *Moleskin for blisters*
- ☐ *Breath mints*
- ☐ *Chapstick*
- ☐ *Insect Repellent, Insect Bite Medication*

- [ ] *Sunblock and Sunburn Relief Lotion*
- [ ] *Dry Skin Lotion/Hand Cream*
- [ ] *Eye Drops or Eye Lubricant*
- [ ] *Saline nasal spray, moisturizing nasal spray*
- [ ] *Vitamins*
- [ ] *Prescription drugs*

NOTE: These should be kept in their original pharmacy containers which provide both drug and doctor information. Be sure to note the drug's generic name. You will want to pack these in your carry on baggage in case the bags you've checked become lost or delayed.

- [ ] *Condoms or prescription birth control*
- [ ] *Physicians' names, addresses, and telephone numbers*
- [ ] *Health Insurance phone numbers*
  NOTE: Be sure to contact your provider to find out about coverage while traveling in the U.S. and abroad.
- [ ] *Names and phone numbers of people to contact in case of an emergency.*

*P*ACKING

*C*HECKLIST

CARRY ON BAGGAGE:

☐ Travelers' First Aid Kit (see above)

☐ Wallet (credit cards, traveler's checks)

☐ Jewelry and other sentimental and valuable items that you feel you *must* bring

☐ Identification (Passport, Driver's License or Photo ID)

☐ Photocopies of the following Important Documents:

☐ Hotel/resort street address, phone number, written confirmation of arrangements and reservations

☐ Complete travel itinerary

☐ Airline tickets

- ☐ Name, address and phone number of emergency contact person(s) back home

- ☐ Medicine prescriptions (including generic names) and eyeglass prescription information (or an extra pair); list of food and drug allergies

- ☐ Phone numbers (including after-hour emergency phone numbers) for health insurance company and personal physicians

- ☐ Copy of your packing list. This will help you while packing up at the end of your trip. It will also be invaluable if a piece of your luggage gets lost, as you will know the contents that are missing.

- ☐ List of your travelers checks' serial numbers and 24 hour phone number for reporting loss or theft

- ☐ Phone numbers to the local U.S. embassy or consulate

- ☐ Any "essential" toiletries and one complete casual outfit in case checked baggage is delayed or lost

- ☐ Foreign language dictionary or translator

❑ Camera with film loaded

❑ Maps

❑ Phone numbers to the local US embassy or consulate

❑ Small bills/change (in U.S. dollars and in the appropriate foreign currency) for tipping

❑ Currency converter chart or pocket calculator

❑ Reading material

❑ Eyeglasses

❑ Contact lenses

❑ Contact lens cleaner

❑ Sunglasses

❑ Kleenex, gum, breath mints, and any over-the-counter medicine to ease travel discomfort

❑ Inflatable neck pillow (for lengthy, sit down travels)

❑ Address book and thank you notes (in case you have lots of traveling time)

❑ This Book

❑ Your Budget Sheet

Other items to carry-on ...

☐ _____

☐ _____

☐ _____

☐ _____

☐ _____

☐ _____

☐ _____

CHECKED BAGGAGE:

Clothing:

☐ *Casual wear* (Consider the number of each casual outfit item that you will need)

    ☐ shorts

    ☐ pants

    ☐ tops

    ☐ jackets/sweaters

    ☐ sweatshirts/sweatsuits

    ☐ belts

    ☐ socks

    ☐ underwear or panties & bras

    ☐ walking shoes/sandals/loafers

    ☐ _____

☐ *Athletic wear* (Consider the number of each sporting outfit item that you will need)

    ☐ shorts

    ☐ sweatpants

    ☐ tops

    ☐ sweatshirts/jackets

    ☐ swim suits

    ☐ swim suit cover-up

    ☐ aerobic activity outfit

    ☐ athletic equipment

    ☐ hats

    ☐ socks

    ☐ underwear or panties & exercise bras

    ☐ tennis/athletic shoes

    ☐ _____

    ☐ _____

☐ *Evening wear* (Consider the number of each evening outfit item that you will need)

    ☐ pants or pants/skirts/dresses

    ☐ belts

    ☐ dress shirts/blouses

- ☐ sweaters
- ☐ jackets/blazers/ties
- ☐ socks or pantyhose/slips
- ☐ underwear or panties & bras
- ☐ accessories
- ☐ shoes
- ☐ _____
- ☐ _____

☐ *Formal wear* (Consider the number of each formal outfit item that you will need)

- ☐ dress pants/suits/tuxedo
- ☐ dresses/gowns
- ☐ dresses
- ☐ accessories
- ☐ socks or pantyhose/slips
- ☐ underwear or panties & bras
- ☐ dress shoes
- ☐ _____
- ☐ _____

☐ *Other Clothing items*

- ☐ pajamas

- ☐ lingerie
- ☐ slippers
- ☐ robe
- ☐ _____
- ☐ _____

Miscellaneous items:

- ☐ An additional set of the important document photocopies as packed in your carry on
- ☐ Travel tour books, Tourism Bureau Information numbers
- ☐ Journal
- ☐ Special honeymoon gift for your new spouse
- ☐ Any romantic items or favorite accessories
- ☐ Extra film and camera batteries
- ☐ Plastic bags for dirty laundry
- ☐ Large plastic or nylon tote bag for bringing home new purchases
- ☐ Small sewing kit and safety pins
- ☐ Travel alarm clock
- ☐ Travel iron
- ☐ Lint brush

- ☐ Compact umbrella
- ☐ Fold up rain slickers
- ☐ Hand held tape recorder (for recorded memory journal or for bringing along your favorite, romantic tapes) and/or videocamera
- ☐ _____
- ☐ _____

For International travel:

- ☐ Passports/visas
- ☐ Electric converters and adapter plugs
- ☐ Copy of appropriate forms showing proof of required vaccinations/inoculations
- ☐ _____
- ☐ _____

Other items to bring ...

- [ ] _____
- [ ] _____
- [ ] _____
- [ ] _____
- [ ] _____
- [ ] _____
- [ ] _____
- [ ] _____
- [ ] _____
- [ ] _____
- [ ] _____
- [ ] _____
- [ ] _____
- [ ] _____
- [ ] _____
- [ ] _____
- [ ] _____
- [ ] _____
- [ ] _____
- [ ] _____

Items to leave behind (with a trusted contact person) ...

❏ Photocopy of all travel details (complete itineraries, names, addresses, and telephone numbers)

❏ Photocopy of credit cards along with 24 hour telephone number to report loss or theft. (Be sure to get the number to call when traveling abroad. It will be a different number than their U.S. 1-800 number.)

❏ Photocopy of travelers checks along with 24 hour telephone number to report loss or theft

❏ Photocopy of passport identification page, along with date and place of issuance

❏ Photocopy of drivers license

❏ Any irreplaceable items

*I*NTERNATIONAL

*T*RAVEL

There are over 250 U.S. embassies and consulates around the world. After contacting the Tourism Bureau for the area you will be traveling to, it is also a wise idea to contact the U.S. Embassy or Consulate for that region. With assistance from both of these sources you will be able to determine the travel requirements and recommendations for your chosen travel destination. Within this section you will find numerous resources to assure all of your questions and concerns are addressed before you travel.

Call for a list of U.S. embassy and consulate locations with emergency phone numbers:

(202) 647-5225
or visit: http://travel.state.gov

Personal

Notes

$\mathscr{P}$ASSPORTS AND

$\mathscr{V}$ISAS

Your travel agent should be able to provide you with information to adequately prepare you for your international travels. Additional information (and possibly more detailed and current information) can be obtained by contacting the appropriate sources listed in this section.

As a U.S. citizen, you generally need a passport to enter and to depart most foreign countries and to reenter the United States. Some countries also require Visas. A Visa is an endorsement by officials of a foreign country as permission to visit their country. You first need a passport in order to obtain a Visa. Inquire with the resources listed in this section for requirements of your specific destination.

As mentioned, you will be required to prove your U.S. citizenship upon reentry to the

United States. If the country of your destination does not require you to possess a current passport, you will still need to produce proof of citizenship for U.S. Immigration. Items that are acceptable as proof of citizenship include a passport, a certified copy of your Birth Certificate, a Certificate of Nationalization, a Certificate of Citizenship, or a Report of Birth Abroad of a Citizen of the United States. Proof of identification can include a driver's license or a government or military identification card containing a photo or physical description.

NOTE: Your fiancée should have her passport and airline tickets reflect her maiden name for ease in proof of identification while traveling. Name changes can be processed after returning from the honeymoon with your marriage certificate.

Your passport will be one of the most important documents you will take with you. Contact the local U.S. Embassy immediately if your passport becomes lost or stolen. Have a photocopy of your passports' data page, date and place of issuance, and passport number to be kept with a contact person at home. You should also travel with a set of these photocopies in addition to an extra set of loose passport photos for speed in attaining a replacement.

Passports can be obtained from one of the 13 U.S. Passport Agencies (listed later in this section) or one of the thousands of authorized passport locations, such as state and federal courts as well as some U.S. Post Offices (check in the Government Listings section of your phone book).

Currently, the cost to obtain a passport is $65.00 (in person; Form DSP-11) or $55.00 (through the mail; Form DSP-82). If you have had a passport in the past, contact a passport agency to find out if you are eligible to apply through the mail. You will want to apply for your passport several months before your trip, keeping in mind that January through July is a busier time and the process may take longer.

In addition to calling the U.S. Passport Agencies for personal assistance, you can also call their 24-hour recorded information lines for information on agency locations, travel advisories and warnings, and Consular Information Sheets pertaining to every country in the world.

Travel Advisory Updates are also available 24 hours a day by calling:

 The Department of State's Office
 of Overseas Citizens' Services at:
 (202) 647-5225

Additional, and very helpful, official information for U.S. citizens regarding international travel can be found at:
> http://travel.state.gov

Foreign embassies and consulates located in the U.S. can provide current information regarding their country. You can locate phone numbers and addresses in the following:
> *The Congressional Directory*
> *Foreign Consular Offices in the*
> *United States*
> (both available at your local library)

U.S. Passport Agencies
http://travel.state.gov/passport_services.html
800-688-9889

Boston Passport Agency

Inquiries:	(617) 565-6990
24-hr Info. Line:	(617) 565-6698

Chicago Passport Agency

Inquiries:	(312) 341-6020
24-hr Info. Line:	(312) 341--6020

Honolulu Passport Agency

Inquiries:	(808) 522-8283
24-hr Info. Line:	(808) 522-8283

Houston Passport Agency

Inquiries:	(713) 751-0294
24-hr Info. Line:	(713) 751-0294

Los Angeles Passport Agency
Inquiries: (310) 235-7075
24-hr Info. Line: (310) 235-7070
Miami Passport Agency
Inquiries: (305) 859-2705
24-hr Info. Line: (305) 859-2705
New Orleans Passport Agency
Inquiries: (504) 412-2600
24-hr Info. Line: (504) 512-2600
New York Passport Agency
Inquiries: (212) 374-0615
24-hr Info. Line: (212) 374-0615
Philadelphia Passport Agency
Inquiries: (215) 597-7480
24-hr Info. Line: (215) 597-7480
San Francisco Passport Agency
Inquiries: (415) 744-5627
24-hr Info. Line: (415) 538-2700
Seattle Passport Agency
Inquiries: (206) 808-5700
24-hr Info. Line: (206) 808-5700
Stamford Passport Agency
Inquiries: (203) 969-9000
24-hr Info. Line: (203) 969-9000
Washington Passport Agency
Inquiries: (202) 647-0518
24-hr Info. Line: (202) 647-0518

Some private sources offering assistance in obtaining a passport (usually offering expedited service):

International Visa Service
    1 (888) 847-2778
World Wide Visas
    1 (800) 833-5423
Travel Document Systems
    1 (800) 874-5100
    www.traveldocs.com

ℋEALTH

𝒞ONCERNS

In the United States the National Center for Infectious Diseases (NCID) and the Centers for Disease Control (CDC) provide the most current information pertinent to international travel. The World Health Organization (WHO) concerns itself with general and specific health issues for almost every part of the world. Health and safety issues as related to international travel are the basis for the International Heath Regulations adopted by the World Health Organization.

Your travel agent should be fully informed about current conditions and requirements. Your personal physician should also be able to provide you with health-related information and advice for traveling in the region you visit. You can personally obtain very useful (and very thorough) information by using the appropriate sources listed below:

Available from the Center for Disease Control and Prevention, Travelers' Health Section:

Health Information for International Travel *("The Yellow Book")*
>available from:
>The Superintendent of Documents
>U.S. Government Printing Office
>Washington, D.C. 20402
>202-512-1800
>or download a free copy at:
>www.cdc.gov

Summary of Health Information for International Travel *("The Blue Sheet")*
>A biweekly publication
>available by fax:
>404-332-4565 (request
>document 220022#)

For updates and changes by phone or fax:
>(404) 332-4559
>or visit: www.cdc.gov

OTHER CONCERNS

TRAVELERS' HEALTH INSURANCE COVERAGE

If your health insurance policy does not cover you abroad, consider acquiring a temporary health insurance policy. Travel agencies, health insurance companies, travelers' check companies, and your local phone book should be able to provide names of relevant companies for you. In addition to health insurance coverage, many policy packages also include protection in case of trip cancellation and baggage loss.

CUSTOMS

Keep prescription medications in their original pharmacy containers with the original labels. Bring a copy of your prescriptions and note the drug's generic name. You may consider getting a letter from your physician warranting your need for the medication.

Some useful publications regarding customs and custom policies:

Know Before You Go; Customs Hints for Returning U.S. Residents
> U.S. Customs
> P.O. Box 7407
> Washington, D.C. 20004
> 202-566-8195

Travelers' Tips on Bringing Food, Plant and Animal Products into the United States
> U.S. Department of Agriculture
> 613 Federal Building
> 6505 Belcrest Road
> Hyattsville, MD 20782

An Unwanted Souvenir; Lead in Ceramic Ware
> U.S. Food and Drug Administration
> HFI-40
> Rockville, MD 20857

*T*HINGS TO DO

FOR YOUR HONEYMOON

DONE

Things to do

FOR YOUR HONEYMOON

DONE

THINGS TO DO
FOR YOUR HONEYMOON

DONE

Things to do

FOR YOUR HONEYMOON

DONE

*T*HINGS TO DO
FOR YOUR HONEYMOON

DONE

*T*HINGS TO DO

FOR YOUR HONEYMOON

DONE

WEDDING WS SOLUTIONS
publishing incorporated

proudly presents ...

YOUR BRIDAL SUPERSTORE

...everything but the groom[SM]

www.YourBridalSuperstore.com

...offering the largest selection of the most beautiful and unique wedding accessories, jewelry, invitations and gifts available. Find everything you need for your wedding in one convenient location!

Also Featuring...

→ Advice From Wedding
   Planning Experts

→ Tips to Save Money

→ On Line Classified Section

→ Chat Room

→ And Much More

FREE * **Wedding Planning Software when you visit**

www.YourBridalSuperstore.com

* You pay only shipping and handling

The following wedding checklist
includes a list of some of the items
currently available at

www.YourBridalSuperstore.com

Wedding
Checklist

Wedding Stationery

- ❏ Invitations / Envelopes
- ❏ Announcements
- ❏ Reception Enclosures
- ❏ Respond Cards / Envelopes
- ❏ At Home Cards
- ❏ Programs
- ❏ Book Marks
- ❏ Thank You Notes
- ❏ Calligraphy Pens
- ❏ Pew Cards
- ❏ Decorative Seals
- ❏ Lined Inner Envelopes
- ❏ Printed Envelopes
- ❏ Bows, Ribbons, Wraps

YOUR BRIDAL
SUPERSTORE
...everything but the groom℠

Reception Essentials

- ❏ Cake Knife & Server
- ❏ Tissue Bells, Streamers
- ❏ Cake Boxes or Bags
- ❏ Book or Box Matches
- ❏ Favor Making Supplies
- ❏ Candy Hearts
- ❏ Place Cards
- ❏ Ribbon Pulling Charms
- ❏ Bouquet Holders
- ❏ Favor Ribbons
- ❏ Candy Bar Wrapper Favors
- ❏ Glass Candle Favors
- ❏ Cake Tops
- ❏ Cake Top Domes
- ❏ Floating Candles / Glass Cylinder
- ❏ Favor Bells
- ❏ Toasting Glasses / Goblets
- ❏ Wedding Bubbles
- ❏ Sequined / Chiffon Heart Tie Ons
- ❏ "Just Married" Banner
- ❏ Biodegradable Heart Shaped Rice
- ❏ Seeds of Love
- ❏ Balloons

Wedding Party Gifts

- ❏ Personalized Glassware and Flask
- ❏ Keepsake Box
- ❏ Rich Vanilla Candle
- ❏ Jewelry Heart Box
- ❏ Flower Girl T-Shirt / Coloring Book
- ❏ Ring Bearer T-Shirt / Coloring Book
- ❏ Flower Girl Teddy Bear
- ❏ Ring Bearer Teddy Bear
- ❏ Bridesmaid Photo Mat
- ❏ Heart-Shaped Compact
- ❏ Maid of Honor Appreciation Card
- ❏ Groomsman / Best Man Mugs
- ❏ Keepsake Money Clip
- ❏ Pen and Light w / Case
- ❏ Cherrywood and Pewter Box
- ❏ Bridesmaid Calendar

Ceremony Essentials

- ❏ Aisle Runner
- ❏ Unity Candle
- ❏ Taper Candles

YOUR BRIDAL SUPERSTORE
...everything but the groom℠
www.YourBridalSuperstore.com

Ceremony Essentials *(con't.)*

- ❏ Guest Book
- ❏ Plume Pen
- ❏ Gratuity Envelopes
- ❏ Wedding Programs
- ❏ Pew Bows
- ❏ Wedding Votive Candles
- ❏ Flower Girl Basket
- ❏ Ring Bearer Pillow

Special Items

- ❏ Parent's Gifts
- ❏ Memories Box
- ❏ Marriage Certificate
- ❏ Thank You Guide
- ❏ Personalized License Plate
- ❏ Car Decorating Kit
- ❏ Glass Chalk
- ❏ Bridal Gown Cover
- ❏ Video Case
- ❏ Wedding Time Capsule
- ❏ Gold Engravable Hearts

YOUR BRIDAL
SUPERSTORE
...everything but the groom℠